The Essential DIY Wedding Planner

Alison McNicol

First published in 2014 by Kyle Craig Publishing

Text and illustration copyright © 2014 Kyle Craig Publishing

Design: Julie Anson

ISBN: 978-1-908707-54-3

A CIP record for this book is available from the British Library.

A Kyle Craig Publication

www.kyle-craig.com

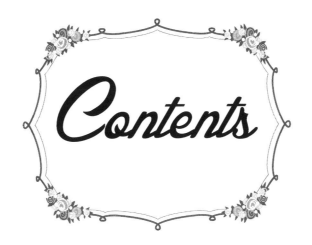

Contents

Introduction

Welcome to the Essential DIY Wedding Planner book!

Congratulations!

You're engaged, and planning your wedding! This is going to be one of the most exciting times of your life, and this book is here to help you every step of the way as you plan your big day. How exciting!

Right now, you're probably not sure where to start – there's just so much to think about!

Perhaps you're wondering just what you should be doing, and how far in advance? How much to budget for each part of your wedding, who to invite, where to hold it, what sort of theme you might like, or simply how to go about finding the right photographer?

Or maybe you still can't decide whether to go down the traditional route or do something a little bit different?

Fear not, this book will cover it all, and more. PLUS – lots of top tips and advice from real brides who share experiences from their own big days – what do they wish they'd done differently, and what were their best big day decisions!

From choosing the right dress to making sense of all the legal requirements, you'll find answers to all of those big questions (and the niggly little ones) that you've been puzzling over. We've also included handy checklists for you to fill in as you go along so that you can keep all your thoughts and plans in one place!

So without further ado (or should that be, I do?) let's get started!

Alison x

The First Questions
When, Where, Who, How?

The first thing you need to do once you've said that all-important 'yes' is to let friends and family know your amazing news. Needless to say it's always best to tell both sets of parents before anyone else. If they find out via Facebook/Aunt Ethel/Mrs Dawson at the post office, they'll be less than pleased. Make them the priority, tell them first and then you can tell the rest of the world.

Once you've let the dust settle and enjoyed the excitement of announcing your engagement, it's time to think about actually getting married some day! Do you want a long or short engagement? Summer or winter wedding? Do you need lots of time to save, or want to get married right away?

Let's take a look at some of the first things to discuss with your fiancé to make sure you are both on the same page. Grab and pen and your partner and start making notes!

The... When?

What time of year do you want to get hitched?

Spring, so beautiful and bright, evocative of fresh starts and new beginnings. Themes of daisies and snowdrops and fresh cut green grass. For an Easter wedding you could have a giant chocolate egg as the wedding cake and an Easter egg hunt for all of the kids after the wedding breakfast.

Or what about a **Summer** date with white lace tables and rustic buckets of pink roses at the centre? Sensual summer allows balmy nights under a marquee, and the party doesn't need to end so early. A couple I know once held their wedding at a summer festival. The couple had pre-booked a marquee space in amongst the festival tents, and then all the guests camped in the main campsite. The party went on all weekend and the entertainment was all ready-made at the festival.

Autumn is fabulous for a cosy and colourful wedding feel – either at home or abroad. There's nothing like the UK, or even New York or America's East coast in the 'fall'. It's still warm but you have the golden colours of September burning into the tangerine hues of October. In Italy it's still warm but comfortable, unlike scorching July, and the same goes for Greece, Spain and other parts of Europe too.

A **Winter** wedding? Avoid booking a date too close to Christmas as it's a stressful time for most people and you want your guests and wedding party to be as relaxed as possible. Only book a wedding close to these dates if you are having minimal preparation done by yourselves or if you have no other work or family commitments. That said, the wonderful thing about a wedding over the holidays is that most venues are already dressed for Christmas, therefore your decorations could be very minimal, if you're happy with what is already provided. Some couples actually prefer a Christmas wedding as it's a time when families aim to come together anyway, so this provides the perfect focus for fun and festivities!

The... Where?

Church or Civil Service?

Do you want to have your actual ceremony in a church, or in the same venue as your reception? If you are religious then a church ceremony will probably be your best choice. Many people marry in their own local church, but you might want to marry in a church away from where you live because it has special significance for you. If this is the case, bear in mind that you will need to make many trips to the church – and if it is far away this can be quite a demanding commitment in the weeks and months running up to your wedding.

The first step is to contact the vicar at the church of your choice and he can talk you through the requirements.

You can marry in a CofE church if you can show:-

That one of you:

- has at any time lived in the parish for a period of at least 6 months or
- was baptised in the parish concerned or
- was prepared for confirmation in the parish or
- has at any time regularly gone to normal church services in the parish church for a period of at least 6 months or

That one of your parents, at any time after you were born:

- has lived in the parish for a period of at least 6 months or
- has regularly gone to normal church services in the parish church for a period of at least 6 months

or that one of your parents or grandparents was married in the parish.

Most Church of England marriages require *banns* to be read out in church before the wedding can take place.

- Banns are an announcement in church of your intention to marry, and an opportunity for anyone to say why the marriage may not lawfully take place.
- Banns are an ancient legal tradition and have been read out every week in churches across the land for millions of couples, over many centuries.
- Banns need to be read in the parish where each of you lives as well as the church in which you are to be married, if that is somewhere else.
- You must have your banns read out in church for three Sundays during the three months before the wedding. This is often done over three consecutive Sundays but does not have to be. This is usually when you will be required to attend the service.

Civil Ceremonies

Of course, marrying in a church isn't essential and as well as marrying in your local Registry Office, lots of hotels and venues have their own licenses to conduct weddings on the premises too.

The first step is to register your intent to marry at your local registry office. You can do this no more than a year in advance of your wedding date, but no less than 22 days before. You will then both be asked to attend a meeting, and bring a variety of documents with you. If you wish to book a registrar to marry you in a licensed venue, it's important to make sure they are available on the date you require before you commit to the venue, and vice versa.

If you're thinking about marrying abroad then visit their national website for information on the relevant documents you will require. Check to see if the ceremonies there are considered legal when you return home. Sometimes you'll need to have a civil service back home to make it count on paper.

The Venue

Do you dream of a country house hotel, with a sweeping gravel driveway, stunning gardens and amazing period features – a scene straight out of Downtown Abbey? Or perhaps you've always dreamt of a small, intimate wedding at home – a marquee in the garden and a small group of family and friends present? Or maybe you imagine a more traditional set-up – a service in the local church that your family have attended for years, followed by a classy recep-

tion in a local hotel or venue, all close to home. Or maybe you have other ideas? Barefoot on the beach? A sun-soaked Spanish finca? A cool city wedding in a modern venue with a rooftop bar? Now is the time to brainstorm with your fiancé and figure out what sort of wedding you're both happy with.

The...How?

What's your Budget?

If you want to get married you can do it for the cost of the license and not much else. Weddings are created on budgets from £200-£200,000 and there's joy and beauty in every one, irrespective of the money spent. That said, it's important that you and your partner set yourselves a budget limit, otherwise you could quickly lose track of costs.

Is anyone likely to help you with the costs? Or would you rather pay for it yourselves? Is a loan an option? It's best not to presume that you're parents will assist you financially but if you have a good relationship with your families then there's no harm in asking for a helping hand.

Maybe you've been saving and have a wedding fund? Well done if so, you are very practical. Credit cards can be tempting, but consider whether you really want to spend the first few years of married life paying off wedding debts!

Should You Have A Theme?

Lots of couples choose a theme to tie their wedding day together – something personal to the two of you that will make the day completely 'you' !

A well-travelled couple could have a 'world' theme – with each table named after a place they've visited…. a cool, rock & roll couple might go for a music theme, naming tables after their favourite songs…will you two have a theme? Or are you happy with a more traditional wedding setting, and will perhaps choose a particular colour as the thread that ties each element of your big day together? Rustic shades for an Autumn wedding, with hand-tied raffia floral arrangements? Spring flowers and daisies in Spring? A seaside/ice-cream theme for a hot, summer beach wedding? What will your wedding 'feel' be?

The... Who?

Who will you invite? Size does matter. Both financially and emotionally. How many guests you invite to the ceremony in particular is a pivotal question which can then dictate the reception venue, menu and the budget. But whether your budget is big or small, with some careful planning and a bit of creativity you can have just as beautiful a day on any budget!

Discuss with your partner what each of you consider to be the 'absolute essentials' and what sort of ideas you both have for fun extras, the 'fun potentials', if budget allows.

GUESTS

MY SIDE

Mum	Jess
Dad	Marcu
Jen	Toby
Richard	Evie
Ruth	Tom
Grandma	Rebec
Auntie Helen	Loui:
Uncle Rob	Craig
Auntie Maddy	Lesli
Uncle Pete	Cam
Katie	Holl
Layla	Ada

	Absolute Essentials	*Fun Potentials*
Wedding Date		
Location		
Theme		
Venue		
Guest List Size		
Entertainment		
Finishing Touches		
Flowers		
Food & Drink		
Cake		
Photography/Video		
Transportation		
Honeymoon		
Other		
Other		
Other		

Your
Wedding
Timeline

Once you have decided on each aspect of your big day, it's really helpful to have a timeline to stick to so you can ensure things run smoothly and everything gets done on time. Once you have read through the whole book and decided on everything, you can return to these pages regularly and fill in the checklist as you go along.

Here is a rough breakdown of what to do and when:

A year before

- Work out exactly what you have to spend budget wise.
- Decide what kind of service you want – civil or church and if you want to marry at home or abroad.
- Create a draft guest list (you can always alter this later). You will need this rough idea of numbers when talking to venues and getting quotes.
- Set your date and time for the ceremony and reserve your chosen venue.
- Look through wedding magazines for dress inspiration, and have a day out with friends or family to try on some dresses.
- Decide where you're going to have your wedding gift list and start choosing your dream presents (this is the really fun part!). If you would rather guests contributed to your honeymoon or another fund, set up a separate bank account for people to pay into.
- Book a photographer, and a videographer if you want one. Or if you're on a tight budget, see if a friend can do the videoing for you.
- Reserve your band or DJ, or if you're going to do the music yourself start putting together your dream playlist and ask friends and family for suggestions. Doing little things like that now will save time later and you can add to it nearer the time.

Eight months before

- Send out save the date cards or, if you're on a tight budget, email everyone or set up a Facebook page and invite your guests to join.
- Choose some hotels with different price points near to the venue for guests who are travelling and see if you can negotiate a discounted rate for a block booking.
- Buy your dress so you've got time for several fittings over the coming months. Also choose your shoes so the height of your dress can be tailored accordingly.
- Start planning your honeymoon and ensure you've got plenty of time left on your passports.

Six months before

- Once you've made a definite decision on your colour scheme, choose and book your florist.
- Start planning your dream wedding cake and go for some tastings.Decide on the menu for the big day.
- Get your bridesmaids together and go dress shopping so you've for plenty of time for alternations to be made to the outfits.
- Arrange transport for yourself and guests from the ceremony to the reception.
- Send out those all-important wedding invitations! The more time people have to prepare, the better. Set a deadline of a month for people to let you know if they're attending.
- Choose your wedding rings and get any alternations done.
- Start planning your hen and stag parties.

Three months before

- Put together the seating plan.
- Write a complete plan of the day. What time do you want to do the speeches, cut the cake and have the first dance?
- Now you know how many guests are coming, let your venue and caterers know definite numbers and inform them of any special dietary or access requirements.
- Decide on your first dance song.
- Speak to everyone you would like to give a speech or a toast and ensure they're happy to do so.
- Ditto with the readings. Now is the time to choose which readings you would like, and who would you like to read them.
- Meet up with hair and make-up artists to try out different looks. Take a picture of each look so you can compare them later on.
- Order wedding favours, if you're planning to have them.
- Buy your wedding underwear and evening outfit, if you're planning to change during the day.
- Contact anyone who has not yet RSVP'd.
- Buy gifts for the bridesmaids, ushers and best man.

One month before

- Finalise your playlist, or give an updated version of songs you'd like played to your band or DJ.
- Meet up with your photographer (and videographer if you have one) to talk through your requirements and any specific shots you're like.
- Get your marriage license. Don't forget this one!
- Have your final dress fitting and start to wear your shoes around the house to break them in.

	Decide On & Book	Decision
12 months	Budget	
	Church or Civil?	
	Draft Guest List	
	Wedding Date	
	Venue(s)	
	Dress ideas	
	Gift List	
	Photographer	
	Band or DJ	
	Any other entertainment/ extras	
	Transportation	
8 months	Save The Date Cards	
	Guest Hotels List	
	Dress & shoes	
	Honeymoon	

6 months	Colours/theme	
	Flowers	
	Cake	
	Menu	
	Send Invitations	
	Rings	
	Hen & Stag Parties	
3 months	Seating Plan	
	Speeches/Readings	
	Running order of day	
	Confirm numbers & food	
	Hair & make-up tests	
	Wedding favours	
	Bridal Underwear	
	Wedding Party Gifts	
1 month	DJ/Music playlist	
	Meet with photographer	
	Final dress fitting	
	Get Marriage Licence!	

The Final Countdown!

One week before:

- Book any beauty appointments – nail, wax, tan etc.
- Check in with the caterers, entertainment, flowers, transport and cake makers.
- Have your wedding rehearsal.
- Wrap the gifts for the wedding party.
- Check the best man has the wedding rings.
- Ensure your bridesmaids are all happy with their outfits and shoes.
- Confirm who is coming to you, and at what time, to get ready on the day.
- Pack for your honeymoon, buy any last minute essentials and arrange travel money, travellers' cheques or a holiday credit card.
- Give the best man cash for any fees payable on the day, plus a list of tasks and contacts for on the day (see page 124).
- Double confirm who is in charge of what on the day, and give checklists.

One day before:

- Get a manicure/pedicure, eyelashes and any personal waxing done! (Be sure to wax or shave a full day before any spray or fake tanning you have planned).
- Pack a small bag of essentials, including make-up, deodorant, hairspray, etc, and arrange for it to be taken to the reception venue along with any gifts.
- Make sure the cake is delivered to the reception venue (today or tomorrow?)
- Put champagne on ice for tomorrow when getting ready.
- Plan any food or snacks for tomorrow for you and your bridal party– don't forget to eat before you get ready.
- Confirm with car company about tomorrow's arrangements

On the day!

- Give yourself plenty of time to get ready.
- Ensure the buttonholes and bouquets are either collected or delivered.
- Enjoy every moment and have an incredible day!

1 week	Beauty Appointments	
	Check in with all vendors	
	Rehearsal	
	Wrap gifts	
	Bridesmaids	
	Honeymoon essentials	
	Cash, Rings and Checklist to best man	
	On-the-day responsibilities – give checklists	
	Confirm who is arriving and when on the day	
The Day before	Manicure/pedicure	
	On the day essentials bag	
	Check on cake delivery	
	Food & Champagne for bridal party	
	Double check bridal car arrival time	
	Final dress fitting	
	Get Marriage Licence!	

Bride
on a
Budget

By now you are probably raring to go and start checking things off your big to-do list, but before you set your heart on a Vera Wang gown or a castle in Scotland it's time to get realistic about your budget.

The last thing you want to do is be panicking about paying for everything in the run up to your special day, and the brilliant thing is that there are venues and honeymoons to suit everyone's budget. With the average cost of a wedding growing all the time (it's currently around £20,000) and more couples than ever paying for their big day themselves, it's essential to know exactly how much cash you've got to flash.

 Before you start thinking about the kind of wedding you'd like there are lots of things to consider.

Will you be getting any help from relatives?

It's never an easy conversation to have but you really need to know from the word go whether or not your families will be making any kind of contribution as it could make all the difference. Of course you need to be subtle when you ask, but ask as soon as you see a good opportunity!

How much can you save from now until then?

Are you able to set aside a certain percentage of your wages each month to put towards the wedding, say 10%? And are you willing to cut back on going out or buying new clothes until after the wedding? It's a good idea to set up a separate wedding account that you add to regularly. You'll be surprised how much you can pull together in a short time.

Are you happy to compromise to cut costs?

- If you get married mid-week venues are generally a lot cheaper than if you choose a weekend date.
- Don't tell vendors it's a wedding!

Booking a venue and food for a 'family party' can often help you avoid the hefty premiums that vendors add when they know it's your big day!

- Consider a pre-loved/ second hand wedding or bridesmaid dresses. Or find out about sample sales and designer clearances on wedding dresses.
- Hit the high street.

The choice of wedding and bridesmaids dresses at budget prices has never been better. Coast, Monsoon and BHS all do great ranges at a fraction of designer cost. Personalise with ribbons, flowers and veils and you'd never know!

- Why not print your own invitationsat home? There are great websites where you can design your own invites.
- Or opt for beautiful e-vites and cut out the costs of printing and postage altogether!
- Make your own table place cards and table seating chart.
- Ask a friend to make the cake/wedding favours/decorations. They'll probably love being asked to help out.
- Cut down your guest list. Yes, that may sound simplistic but do you really want to invite that couple you met on holiday five years ago and haven't seen since? You'll save a small fortune by strict about who you invite.
- Serve Prosecco, Cava or bucks fizz instead of Champagne. A lot of the cheaper alternatives taste just as good these days and people don't generally mind what they're drinking after they've had a couple!
- Hire all of your wedding party outfits.
- Have your hair done in the morning at your chosen hair salon – much cheaper than them coming to you!
- Create your own playlist instead of paying for a DJ. It's what iPhone's were made for. This can be a great task for the groom or best man!
- Have a pay bar in the evening and skip the evening buffet.

- Or, if the venue allows, bring your own booze!

- Pick a venue that already looks amazing. This can cut the cost of hiring fancy chair covers, tablecloths, floral arrangements and table décor.

- If your party isn't too huge, booking out your favourite restaurant during the day could be a great way to get a great venue and food on a budget!

- Have a daytime reception...

...vows at 11am and lunch at 1pm. This could be much cheaper than booking a venue for an all-day/evening party. If you want to keep the party going, hire a room in a nearby pub for your evening party.

- Have a talented friend visit the flower market and make all your table centrepieces and venue floral arrangements.

- Do your own catering.

Small family wedding?

Low-key party in a local hall or marquee. With all hands on deck, there's no reason why you, your friends and family can't pull together an amazing buffet or wedding supper at a fraction of the price of caterers. Just make sure to delegate set-up so that YOU get to relax on the day itself!

- Let them eat cake! Cake, that is, from the high street. Don't fancy paying £800 for a bespoke wedding cake? M&S and Waitrose do amazing plain white iced cakes – ready for you to personalise with flowers, ribbons or hand-made toppers. You'll save a fortune!

- And…talking of cake…skip the dessert. Often wedding cake goes to waste AND you have to fork out for expensive take-home boxes because everyone is full after their 3 course dinner with dessert. Make the cake the dessert – get the venue to cut, plate and serve it as part of the deal, and you instantly cut your catering costs!

- Hit the road! Do you know a friend with a cool or unusual car? Who needs to pay hundreds for a wedding car for a 15 minute ride when you could rock up in your friend's vintage Merc or cute Beetle? I once used my cute cream Mini – dressed with a huge ribbon and a bow – as the wedding car for my best friend. Everyone loved it, I got to drive her on the biggest day of her life, and she saved a fortune!!

Your Big Day Budget Planner!

Item	Budget	Actual Cost	Deposit/Paid	Balance Outstanding
Stationery:				
Save the date cards				
Wedding invites and RSVP cards				
Order of service				
Menus				
Place cards and seating plan				
Thank you notes				
Stamps				
Wedding Service:				
Marriage licence fee				
Officiant's fee				
Church fees				
Tips				
Transport – Bride				
Transport – Groom				
Transport – Bridal Party				
Transport – Guests				
Reception:				
Venue/marquee hire				
Arrival canapes				
Food				
Toast Drink				
Drinks/Bar				
Decorations (tables/chairs etc.)				
DJ/Band				
Evening Food				
Staff				
Other Entertainment				
Other				
Other				
Cake				

Bridal Party:				
Rings				
Wedding Dress				
Bridal Shoes, Under-wear, Accessories				
Groom – suit & shoes				
Bridesmaids Outfits				
Flower girl/page by outfits				
Best Men suits				
Bridal Beauty:				
Hair trial				
Hair on day				
Make-up				
Nails/wax/tan etc.				
Flowers:				
Bride's bouquet				
Bridesmaid's bou-quets				
Buttonholes/groom				
Church Flowers				
Venue Flowers				
Table centrepieces				
Others:				
Photographer/ Video				
Favours				
Gifts to Bridal party				
Wedding Insurance				
Honeymoon:				
Cost				
Spending money				
Sundries				
Other				
Other				
Other				
Other				
TOTALS:				

The Rings

When thinking about budget, consider how much you want to spend on your wedding rings. They are the one item given to each other on that special day which you will have and hold for the rest of your lives, so they not only need to be aesthetically pleasing but practical as well.

You can pick up a plain wedding band from a high street jewellers for as little as £35. It's likely to be made of a hard, non-precious metal but it will be durable and fit for purpose.

Moving into the softer golds, like 9 carat, you can still find reasonable prices, even under £100. But be mindful that if you are a clumsy or accident prone person a softer gold is more likely to mark.

Higher carat golds and platinum are the most hardy metals as there content is purer (ie. not mixed with other metals) and subsequently the price **will be higher**.

If you have your heart set on a ring from a high end store like Tiffany or Cartier then see if you can get a friend or relative to purchase it from America when on holiday because the prices are a lot lower. For example one wedding band in Tiffany London costs £600, the same one in New York costs $600. Depending on the exchange rate at the time of purchase that could be up to half price!

If it's quality you're after but you don't care about the designer label then head to London's Hatton Garden. It's Britain's most famous jewellery quarter and the epicentre for diamonds. You'll find row upon row of top quality jewellery stores selling at near-trade prices.

If you're planning on having the inside of your bands engraved, be sure to plan ahead.

Also – most brides and grooms have their final 'ring fitting' a few weeks before the big day – this is especially important if either of you plans to lose weight in the run up to the big day. You don't want to end up with a ring that is too loose!

Your
Wedding
Ceremony

What kind of Ceremony is right for you?

There are lots of different options when it comes to choosing what's going to be right for you when you walk down the aisle

Church or civil?

It's totally up to you whether you choose a civil or church wedding. Church weddings are more formal and you are expected to wear traditional wedding clothing, whereas pretty much anything goes at a civil ceremony!

Religious ceremonies usually require you to follow the traditional order of service, but of course you can make it more personal to you by choosing readings and music that you love.

If you are religious, of the same faith, and neither you or your partner has been married before, a church ceremony is usually the way to go. However, if you want your nuptials to be more laid back, there's a lot to be said for civil ceremonies. Not only can have the wedding and reception in the same venue if it is licensed for weddings, it's also possible to write your own vows.

Civil weddings are also cheaper with the only charges being the venue hire, officiant's fee, marriage license fee and registration fees, whereas a religious ceremony involves church rental, services, flowers, music and decorations.

Legal Requirements

To marry in the UK you must be:

- Over 16

- Not closely related!

- Free to marry (i.e. single, widowed or divorced)

What you need to do beforehand:

- Give notice at your local register office.

- You will each be charged £35 and will need to take proof of your name, age and nationality in the form of your passport, driving license, birth certificate, immigration status document or national identity card. You also need to take a bank statement, and a utility or Council Tax bill dated within the last three months as proof of address.

- If you've been married or in a civil partnership before you will also need to take along a decree absolute or final order, or the death certificate of your former partner.

Types of Ceremonies

Traditional: these are usually faith-based tradition based on the religious beliefs of the bride and groom.

Non-denominational: this is a spiritual ceremony that is non-religious but may still include references to God.

Interfaith: where two people of differing religions marry so the ceremony will include readings and rituals pertinent to each faith.

Non-religious: this generally doesn't contain any reference to God or a particular faith.

Themed: if couples have a real passion for something – whether it's theme parks, a period of history or a TV show – they can incorporate the theme into their wedding speeches and clothing.

The Marriage Service - Structure

Introduction
The Welcome
Preface
The Declarations
The Collect
Readings
Sermon
The Marriage
The Vows
The Giving of Rings
The Proclamation
The Blessing of the Marriage
Registration of the Marriage
Prayers
The Dismissal

Popular Readings

Most church weddings include one or more readings from the Bible. Have a read through a few and see if there are any with words and meanings pertinent to your relationship.

Think about who will read them; your narrators need to have a clear and confident voice, not be too nervous and be flattered by the request rather than horrified at the thought.

The number 1 most popular reading for weddings is this:

1 Corinthians Chapter 13

If I speak in the tongues of mortals and of angels, but do not have love, I am a noisy gong or a clanging cymbal. And if I have prophetic powers, and understand all mysteries and all knowledge, and if I have all faith, so as to remove mountains, but do not have love, I am nothing. If I give away all my possessions, and if I hand over my body so that I may boast, but do not have love, I gain nothing.

Love is patient; love is kind; love is not envious or boastful or arrogant or rude. It does not insist on its own way; it is not irritable or resentful; it does not rejoice in wrongdoing, but rejoices in the truth. It bears all things, believes all things, hopes all things, endures all things.

Love never ends. But as for prophecies, they will come to an end; as for tongues, they will cease; as for knowledge, it will come to an end. For we know only in part, and we prophesy only in part; but when the complete comes, the partial will come to an end.

When I was a child, I spoke like a child, I thought like a child, I reasoned like a child; when I became an adult, I put an end to childish ways. For now we see in a mirror, dimly, but then we will see face to face. Now I know only in part; then I will know fully, even as I have been fully known. And now faith, hope, and love abide, these three; and the greatest of these is love.

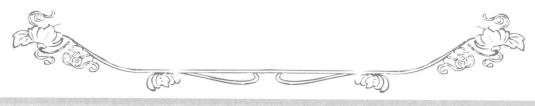

Other passages to consider:

Being a good lover!
(1 John Chapter 4 verses 7-12)

God creates women and men to look after the earth
(Genesis, Chapter 1, verses 26-28)

A love poem between two lovers
(Song of Solomon, Chapter 2, verses 10-13; Chapter 8, verses 6 and 7)

Jesus teaches how to live a life that brings true happiness
(Matthew, Chapter 5, verses 1-10)

Jesus teaches about marriage, and welcomes children
(Mark, Chapter 10, verses 6-9 and 13-16)

What happens when Jesus attends a wedding reception
(John, Chapter 2, verses 1-11)

Committing to each other
(Ephesians Chapter 5, verses 21-33)

Seeing the good side
(Philippians Chapter 4, verses 4-9)

Getting the perfect relationship:

Colossians Chapter 3, verses 12-17

As God's chosen ones, holy and beloved, clothe yourselves with compassion, kindness, humility, meekness, and patience. Bear with one another and, if anyone has a complaint against another, forgive each other; just as the Lord has forgiven you, so you also must forgive. Above all, clothe yourselves with love, which binds everything together in perfect harmony. And let the peace of Christ rule in your hearts, to which indeed you were called in the one body. And be thankful. Let the word of Christ dwell in you richly; teach and admonish one another in all wisdom; and with gratitude in your hearts sing psalms, hymns, and spiritual songs to God. And whatever you do, in word or deed, do everything in the name of the Lord Jesus, giving thanks to God the Father through him.

Popular Hymns

Morning Has Broken

Praise My Soul The King Of Heaven

The Lord's My Shepherd

Lead us Heavenly Father

For The Beauty Of The Earth

The King Of Love My Shepherd Is

Come To A Wedding

O Praise Ye The Lord!

Lord Of The Dance

Make Me A Channel Of Your Peace

One More Step Along The World I Go

Great Is Thy Faithfulness

Lord Of All Hopefulness

As Man And Woman We Were Made

Praise To The Lord, The Almighty

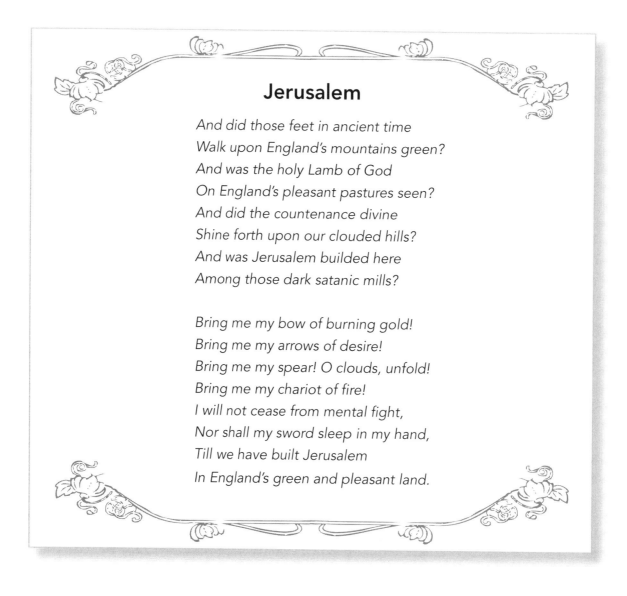

Jerusalem

And did those feet in ancient time
Walk upon England's mountains green?
And was the holy Lamb of God
On England's pleasant pastures seen?
And did the countenance divine
Shine forth upon our clouded hills?
And was Jerusalem builded here
Among those dark satanic mills?

Bring me my bow of burning gold!
Bring me my arrows of desire!
Bring me my spear! O clouds, unfold!
Bring me my chariot of fire!
I will not cease from mental fight,
Nor shall my sword sleep in my hand,
Till we have built Jerusalem
In England's green and pleasant land.

Give Me Joy In My Heart

Give me joy in my heart
Give me joy in my heart, keep me praising,
Give me joy in my heart, I pray;
Give me joy in my heart, keep me praising,
Keep me praising till the break of day.

Sing hosanna, sing hosanna,
Sing hosanna to the King of kings!
Sing hosanna, sing hosanna,
Sing hosanna to the King!

Give me peace in my heart, keep me loving,
Give me peace in my heart, I pray;
Give me peace in my heart, keep me loving,
Keep me loving till the break of day:

Give me love in my heart, keep me serving,
Give me love in my heart, I pray;
Give me love in my heart, keep me serving,
Keep me serving till the break of day:

Sing hosanna, sing hosanna,
Sing hosanna to the King of kings!
Sing hosanna, sing hosanna,
Sing hosanna to the King!

Give me oil in my lamp keep me burning
Give me oil in my lamp, I pray,
Give my oil in my lamp, keep me burning,
Keep me burning 'till the end of day.

Sing hosanna, sing hosanna,
Sing hosanna to the King of kings!
Sing hosanna, sing hosanna,
Sing hosanna to the King!

Give me peace in my heart, keep me resting,
Give me peace in my heart, I pray.
Give me peace in my heart, keep me resting,
Keep me resting 'till the end of day.

Sing hosanna, sing hosanna,
Sing hosanna to the King of kings!
Sing hosanna, sing hosanna,
Sing hosanna to the King!

All Things Bright And Beautiful

All things bright and beautiful
All things bright and beautiful,
All creatures great and small,
All things wise and wonderful,
The Lord God made them all.

Each little flower that opens,
Each little bird that sings,
He made their glowing colours,
He made their tiny wings.

All things bright, etc.

The purple headed mountain,
The river running by,
The sunset, and the morning
That brightens up the sky:

All things bright, etc.

The cold wind in the winter,
The pleasant summer sun,
The ripe fruits in the garden,
He made them every one.

All things bright, etc.

The tall trees in the greenwood,
The meadows where we play,
The rushes by the water
We gather every day:

All things bright, etc.

He gave us eyes to see them,
And lips that we might tell
How great is God Almighty,
Who has made all things well.

Amazing Grace

Amazing Grace
Amazing Grace, how sweet the sound,
That saved a wretch like me,
I once was lost, but now I'm found,
Was blind, but now I see.

'Twas grace that taught my heart to fear,
And grace my fear relieved,
How precious did that grace appear,
The hour I first believed.

Through many dangers, toils and snares
We have already come,
'Twas grace that brought us safe thus far,
And grace will lead us home.

When we've been there ten thousand years,
Bright shining as the sun,
We've no less days to sing God's praise
Than when we first begun.

Amazing Grace, how sweet the sound,
That saved a wretch like me,
I once was lost, but now I'm found,
Was blind, but now I see.

Ceremony Music

You'll want to consider what music to have played whilst the guests gather. This is usually a classical piece like Debussy or Handel. **'The Bridal Chorus'** by **Wagner** is the traditional music for when the Bride walks down the aisle. If you're having a church wedding it's likely these will be your choices but in a civil service you can use whatever you'd like. So have a think about what's important to you and your partner?

My husband decided that he wanted music played as he walked down the aisle so he chose the theme tune to the James Bond movies. I then followed a few minutes later to 'These are a few of my favourite things' from the Sound of Music. It made us all laugh and was an amazing start to the ceremony.

Choirs

You can also book a choir for your wedding at your chosen church. They can be arranged to entertain your guests as they wait for the wedding to start, sing a specific piece of music as chosen by you and your partner or simply boost the voices when it comes to singing the hymns.

If you're having a civil ceremony you can still book a choir to sing for you. Either go through your local church or contact an entertainment agency or local choral group.

Harpist

There's nothing quite as beautiful as a harpist playing as you walk down the aisle. This is a lovely and relatively inexpensive addition because the likelihood is that you will only need the harpist to play for about an hour.

If there's a college nearby why not see if they have any music students who might want the experience and exposure for a smaller fee?

Always audition any musicians you intend to book. Contact them through an entertainment agency or search on the internet for local artists.

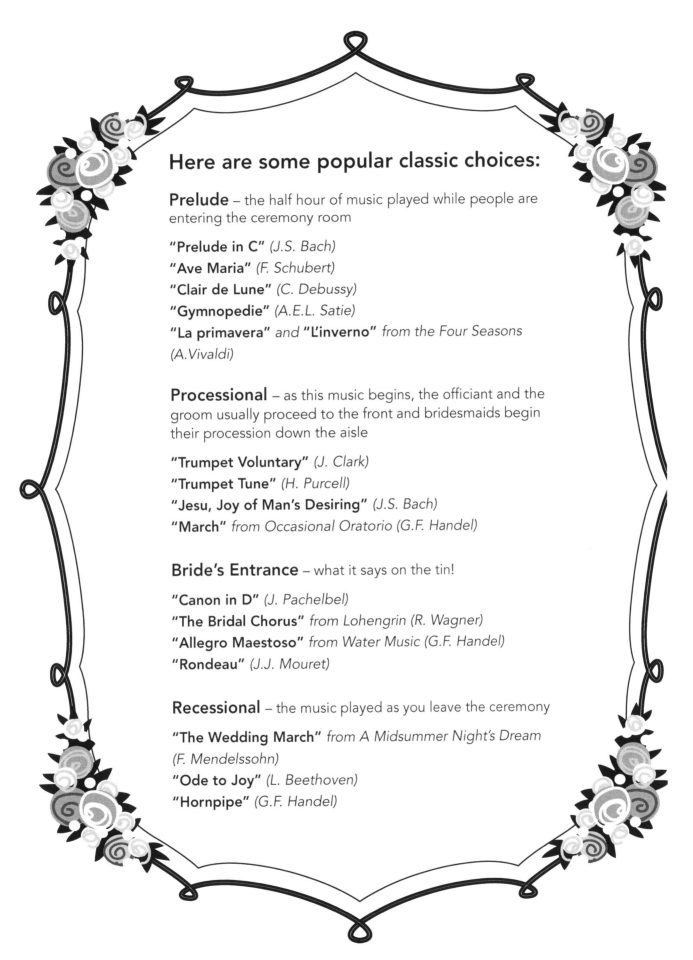

Here are some popular classic choices:

Prelude – the half hour of music played while people are entering the ceremony room

"Prelude in C" (J.S. Bach)
"Ave Maria" (F. Schubert)
"Clair de Lune" (C. Debussy)
"Gymnopedie" (A.E.L. Satie)
"La primavera" and **"L'inverno"** from the Four Seasons (A.Vivaldi)

Processional – as this music begins, the officiant and the groom usually proceed to the front and bridesmaids begin their procession down the aisle

"Trumpet Voluntary" (J. Clark)
"Trumpet Tune" (H. Purcell)
"Jesu, Joy of Man's Desiring" (J.S. Bach)
"March" from Occasional Oratorio (G.F. Handel)

Bride's Entrance – what it says on the tin!

"Canon in D" (J. Pachelbel)
"The Bridal Chorus" from Lohengrin (R. Wagner)
"Allegro Maestoso" from Water Music (G.F. Handel)
"Rondeau" (J.J. Mouret)

Recessional – the music played as you leave the ceremony

"The Wedding March" from A Midsummer Night's Dream (F. Mendelssohn)
"Ode to Joy" (L. Beethoven)
"Hornpipe" (G.F. Handel)

Your
Wedding
Party

The Wedding Party is an essential part of anyone's celebrations, and they play a huge part in ensuring your day runs smoothly.

Whether someone is a bridesmaid, an usher or a maid of honour, a lot of responsibility comes with being a part of the wedding party, so it's always good to give people options when asking them if they would like to play a part in your nuptials. Allow people to bow out gracefully if they decide it isn't for them, and be aware that some people may be worried there will be costs involved so put their minds at ease by tactfully offering to help out with any expenditure.

The size of the wedding party is totally up to you. Some brides choose to have loads of bridesmaids while others may only want a maid of honour. While all grooms have a best man, it's then up to him how many ushers he wants helping out.

While it may balance things out at the reception, the bride and groom don't need to have the same number of attendees.

It's tradition to have children in the wedding party but that doesn't mean you have to have them. In fact, some people choose to have totally child-free weddings so do whatever works best for you.

The Maid Of Honour

The tradition used to be that the bride's sister who was closest in age to her would be her maid of honour (also known as the chief bridesmaid), and if she didn't have a sister another close relative would take on the role. However, times have changed and these days almost anyone can be chosen to be a maid of honour, and they don't always have to be female. Increasingly brothers or male best friends are being asked, and it's not uncommon for a bride to have two or three maids of honour to help her out with the important details in both the run up to the wedding, and on the day itself.

The Maid of Honour's main duties are:
- To accompany the bride on wedding shopping outings.
- To ensure the bridal party are aware of their individual roles.
- To organise a brilliant, fun hen do.
- To help the bride get ready on the wedding day.
- To tend to her veil and train and hold the bouquet during the vows.
- To sign the marriage certificate as a witness.
- To ensure the guests are having a good time.

- To make sure the bride's make-up bag is to hand for touch-ups during the reception.
- Make sure gifts and cards make it safely from the reception the couples' home.
- To be a huge support for the nervous bride throughout!

The Best Man

The best man duties used to go to the groom's brother or another close relative, but nowadays anything goes. It's not unusual for a groom to have a 'best woman' instead of a best man.

The Best Man's main duties are:

- To help out with the groom and usher's tuxedos.
- To organize a great stag do!
- To ensure the groom gets to the church on time.
- To stand by the groom's side and helps to calm his nerves.
- To take care of the weddings rings and sign the marriage certificate.
- To pay the officiant and any other expenses that need settling on the day.
- To check that everyone has transport from the ceremony to the reception.
- To make a funny, emotional and heartfelt speech (no pressure!).
- To send the newlyweds safely on their way once the day has come to an end.
- To arrange for the suits to be returned to the hire shop.

Flower Girls and Ring Bearers

Some couples choose to have young relatives as flower girls and ring bearers. These are usually at least four years old and it's good to bear in that some children can get bored and fidgety when they're away from their parents so they may not always behave as impeccably as you'd like them to! Flower girls walk down the aisle before the bride and sometimes scatter petals, while the ring bearer accompanies her carrying the rings, which he then hands to the best man.

Mother of the Bride

The mother of the bride is usually very involved in both the planning stages and the big day itself.

The mother of the bride's duties are:

- Make a financial contribution towards the wedding.
- Help to choose a dress, shoes and veil for the bride, and the bridesmaid's dresses.

- Help to decide on make-up and hairstyles.
- Help to choose flowers.
- Offer suggestions for the family section of the guest list.
- Make sure the bride has a chilled glass of champagne before the ceremony!

Father of the Bride

The father of the bride's main job is to walk his daughter down the aisle, but he's also got some other important tasks.

The father of the bride's duties are:
- Make a financial contribution towards the wedding.
- Travel to the ceremony with the bride.
- Walk the bride up the aisle.
- Give the first speech and toast the happy couple.
- To dance with his daughter!

Mother and Father of the Groom

It used to be the bride's parents picked up the lion's share of the wedding costs, but these days it's often the norm for the groom's parents to make a contribution as well, should they want to.

Guest Lists
and
Seating Plans

The guest list brings both joy and pain as you will have to decide who from your nearest and dearest attend. If you want to be diplomatic then ask everyone to the whole day, though this can prove expensive.

Don't feel pressured into inviting anyone, especially you or your partner's parents' friends. It's your day, and those precious moments should be for people that you actually know on a one to one basis. The same goes for plus ones. If you want to invite cousins or close work colleagues, fine. But asking them to come solo, as opposed to bringing a plus one that you have never met, will make a huge difference.

If you've got a huge budget and room for everyone then go for it but otherwise trim the fat based on **these questions:**

- Have I spoken to that person in the past six months?
- Did they call or write to congratulate us on our engagement?
- Are you inviting them out of duty?

Most venues have a ceiling limit on the amount of guests able to attend, particularly the ceremony, so this in itself may dictate your numbers. Or you could be tactical and specifically book a smaller venue or church so that your ceremony and wedding breakfast are limited and a little more intimate.

The numbers and the venue can end up being a bit of a chicken and egg situation, which is why knowing your ideal guest lists from the beginning is the best possible scenario. It's really the first thing that requires a firm lockdown.

Ideally you will need three lists:

Daytime (Ceremony and Wedding Breakfast) Guests

Evening Guests – *if you want to invite extras, less close people, for the evening party*

Standby Daytime Guests – *to fill the Daytime places of any 'declines' (see invitation section)*

Children

Some people stipulate a 'no children' policy. This may upset some of your guests (whereas some parents might actually welcome the opportunity to have a day away from their little ones!) but it's your day and you should ultimately do what you want to do. If you do have little people as guests ensure you've told your venue to supply the right amount of high chairs or booster seats. It's also a good idea to provide them with colouring books or small toys to occupy them during the meal.

If you've got children of a variety of ages, the likelihood is that the older ones won't mind looking after the younger ones and so you can create a table just for kids.

It's always a great idea to provide a kids' area where they can not only play during the evening but also crash out on soft seating or bean bags. Have activities such as crafts or a children's entertainer early on and then get a DVD and TV hooked up with favourite films to be played from about 8pm, ideally in a separate kids room. This will help to wind them down.

If you do go for a separate play area it's wise to employ a nanny. This doesn't have to cost the earth and you may even have a friend's teenager who would do it for free.

Planning Your Top Table

The first table to consider when planning your seating is your table, the Top Table!

The traditional top table layout sees the two sets of parents switched so that your mother is sitting beside your groom's father and vice versa, with the chief bridesmaid and best man on each end. However, if the two sets of parents have never met before, you might prefer to seat your parents together. You may also decide to have a family-only top table and seat the best man and chief bridesmaid on a regular table with the other attendants.

A Traditional Top Table

If one or more parents are divorced, the situation can be slightly more complicated, and can depend on family relations, as well as whether one or more parent has a new partner who needs to be included. They can then be seated together, or mixed in with your partner's parents.

Bride's Parents – both with new partners – seated with Groom's parents

Groom's Parents – both with new partners – seated together

If your family is just too complicated or members of the wedding party do not get along, you could simply have a top table for the two of you, and seat parents and their partners on regular tables with other family members.

Sweetheart Table: *A nice compromise can be a 'Sweetheart Table' – where the Bride and Groom have a top table for two, with a table for each side of the wedding party on either side of them.*

Planning Your Seating

Once you have agreed on the final number of guests, the next step is to talk to your venue on the types and number of tables that they have. Or, if you are organizing your own table hire for your own venue or using a marquee, you will want to decide on which tables to use and how to best arrange them. Will you go for round tables or rectangular, or a mix of the two? And how will you lay them out within the space available?

Here are some points to consider:

- What shape is the room?
- Will there be small children at the wedding? If so, will they sit with parents or will you have one or more kids tables?
- All guests will want a good view of the Top Table!
- Keep walkways to the bar, dancefloor and exits clear
- Elderly guests may prefer to be seated close to the nearest toilet exit

Round tables

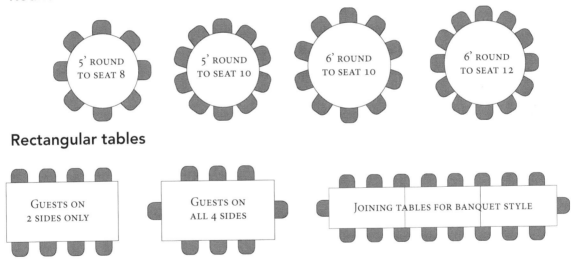

Rectangular tables

Number of Guest Tables	Tables seating 8	Tables Seating 10	Tables seating 12
6	48	60	72
8	64	80	96
10	80	100	120
12	96	120	144
14	112	140	168

Room Layouts - Round Tables

NUMBER OF TABLES	CURVED	STAGGERED	AROUND THE DANCEFLOOR
10	TOP TABLE	TOP TABLE	TOP TABLE
12	TOP TABLE	TOP TABLE	TOP TABLE
14	TOP TABLE	TOP TABLE	TOP TABLE
16	TOP TABLE	TOP TABLE	TOP TABLE
20	TOP TABLE	TOP TABLE	TOP TABLE

NUMBER of TABLES			
10	TOP TABLE	TOP TABLE	TOP TABLE
12	TOP TABLE	TOP TABLE	TOP TABLE
14	TOP TABLE	TOP TABLE	TOP TABLE
16	TOP TABLE	TOP TABLE	TOP TABLE
20	TOP TABLE	TOP TABLE	TOP TABLE

Other Table and Room Layout Ideas

Tables in an E formation

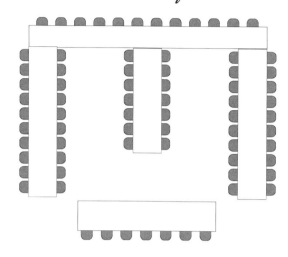

Mix of Tables Cross Shape

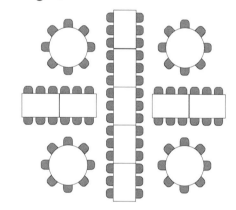

Top Table at Head of Cross Shape

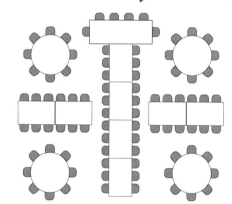

Long Rows of Tables

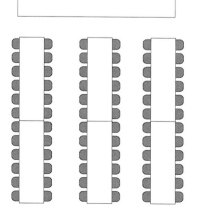

Guest List

Use these pages for the first draft of your potential guest list. Feel free to photocopy in case you need to make several edits!

Bride ~ Family

Groom ~ Family

Bride ~ Family

--------------------   --------------------

--------------------   --------------------

--------------------   --------------------

--------------------   --------------------

--------------------   --------------------

--------------------   --------------------

--------------------   --------------------

--------------------   --------------------

--------------------   --------------------

--------------------   --------------------

--------------------   --------------------

--------------------   --------------------

--------------------   --------------------

--------------------   --------------------

Groom ~ Family

--------------------   --------------------

--------------------   --------------------

--------------------   --------------------

--------------------   --------------------

--------------------   --------------------

--------------------   --------------------

--------------------   --------------------

--------------------   --------------------

--------------------   --------------------

--------------------   --------------------

--------------------   --------------------

--------------------   --------------------

--------------------   --------------------

--------------------   --------------------

Bride ~ Friends

--------------------   --------------------

--------------------   --------------------

--------------------   --------------------

--------------------   --------------------

--------------------   --------------------

--------------------   --------------------

--------------------   --------------------

--------------------   --------------------

--------------------   --------------------

--------------------   --------------------

Groom ~ Friends

--------------------   --------------------

--------------------   --------------------

--------------------   --------------------

--------------------   --------------------

--------------------   --------------------

--------------------   --------------------

--------------------   --------------------

--------------------   --------------------

--------------------   --------------------

--------------------   --------------------

Mutual Friends

--------------------- --------------------- --------------------- ---------------------
--------------------- --------------------- --------------------- ---------------------
--------------------- --------------------- --------------------- ---------------------
--------------------- --------------------- --------------------- ---------------------
--------------------- --------------------- --------------------- ---------------------
--------------------- --------------------- --------------------- ---------------------
--------------------- --------------------- --------------------- ---------------------
--------------------- --------------------- --------------------- ---------------------
--------------------- --------------------- --------------------- ---------------------
--------------------- --------------------- --------------------- ---------------------
--------------------- --------------------- --------------------- ---------------------
--------------------- --------------------- --------------------- ---------------------
--------------------- --------------------- --------------------- ---------------------
--------------------- --------------------- --------------------- ---------------------
--------------------- --------------------- --------------------- ---------------------
--------------------- --------------------- --------------------- ---------------------

Children

--------------------- --------------------- --------------------- ---------------------
--------------------- --------------------- --------------------- ---------------------
--------------------- --------------------- --------------------- ---------------------
--------------------- --------------------- --------------------- ---------------------
--------------------- --------------------- --------------------- ---------------------
--------------------- --------------------- --------------------- ---------------------
--------------------- --------------------- --------------------- ---------------------
--------------------- --------------------- --------------------- ---------------------
--------------------- --------------------- --------------------- ---------------------
--------------------- --------------------- --------------------- ---------------------
--------------------- --------------------- --------------------- ---------------------

Total ---------------------

Gifts

Traditionally china, silver and crystal were given to couples on their wedding day to be used, enjoyed and treasured for a lifetime. The intention was that the 'wedding china' could be used on very special occasions, then passed on to their children and their children's children as family heirlooms. Now obviously tastes have changed, and you may be much more excited at the thought of a cool, chrome Dualit toaster than a cutlery set, but putting together a Gift List for your guests can be one of the most fun parts of the wedding planning!

Gone are the days of receiving 5 kettles and a selection of ugly photo frames. These days it is perfectly acceptable to register for a Gift List at a major store, and provide details to your guests. They can then choose what items from your list fits their budget and buy you both something that they know for sure you want or need.

You can register from anywhere from Tiffany to John Lewis or Not On The High Street, and a good registration lists a wide range of price tags so that each guest can find something within their budget. Your Auntie Sue may be on a tight budget and opt for a £30 salad bowl, whereas rich Uncle Steve may be happy to cough up £199 for that dream espresso machine you've had your eye on!

Simply go into your favourite stores and ask if they can create a wedding list for you. If it's a department store generally they will arm you with a scanning gun and you can whizz around the store zapping what items you like to your heart's content. So much fun! The list will then be made available on the store's website and you will be given a code to distribute to your guests so they can see what you'd like.

The traditional gift list usually consist of items with which to build a home but you may already be living together and have these already. Perhaps you'd rather have guests help towards the cost of your honeymoon, or even a 'buy our first home' fund? No problem – there are tons of websites out there that you can use!

> *www.honeyfund.co.uk*
>
> *www.thebottomdrawer.co.uk*
>
> *www.our-dream-honeymoon.co.uk*
>
> *www.zankyou.com/uk/wedding-lists*
>
> *www.prezola.com*

If you'd rather stick to the traditional wedding lists then this list covers the usual types of gift items. Go through this together and tick the things you definitely need/want and take this with you to the department store, to help you focus and ensure you chose everything you need on the day!

Item	Need?	Item	Need?
Kitchen		**Dining**	
Coffee maker		Champagne flutes	
Toaster		Red wine glasses	
Microwave		White wine glasses	
Bin		Tumblers	
Hand mixer		Dinner plates	
Blender / Nutri-bullet		Side plates	
Ice-cream maker		Bowls	
Cheese board		Napkins	
Food processor		Napkin rings	
Cruett set		Placemats	
Slow cooker		Salad bowl	
Cutlery		Table cloth	
Jug		Other:	
Frying pans		**Bathroom**	
Juicer		Towels	
Kettle		Bath mat	
Saucepans		Soap dispenser etc.	
Mugs		Other:	
Washing machine		**General**	
Dishwasher		Digital radio	
Other:		Garden tools	
Bedroom		Plants	
Sheets		TV	
Duvet set		Vases	
Pillows		Candles	
Mattress Topper		Candlesticks	
Throw		Wine	
Cushions		Picture frames	
Bedside lamps		Pictures	
Other:		Ornaments	
Other:		Cushions/ throws	

Invitations & Stationery

With so many styles and designs to choose from, it can be hard to know where to start when it comes to your invitations and wedding stationery in general.

Your invitations should ideally reflect the theme or colours of your big day. Usually this design will be constant throughout all wedding stationery, from save the date cards, to the main invitations, through to the orders of service, menus and place names and thank you cards.

Invitations come in a variety of different designs to suit any style. Each design can be personalised to suit your individuality. The stationery can incorporate photographs and wording chosen by you to create a one of a kind product which replicates your taste, colour preferences, theme and overall vision.

Your wedding stationery is the first glimpse that your guests will have of your event so you want to make it as evocative and beautiful as the big day itself.

Ask yourself these questions to get started:

1. What's our deadline for sending the invitations?
2. Do we want to hand make everything, buy off the shelf or employ a designer to assist us?
3. If we print everything ourselves is our printer good enough and reliable enough?
4. What's our budget?

The most important thing to remember about any stationery is that it needs to have the right information on it. Check it once, check it three times. Have at least two other people proof read it for spelling mistakes and also missing information. It's quite common to miss off really important items. Read on to see what information is required on each piece of communication you send to guest.

Not sure what sort of style you fancy? Here are some examples:

Traditional
Matching Sets of Wedding Stationery

Modern

Sweet and Simple

Classic and Bold

Themed
– Jack & Rose's Summer Garden Wedding

Themed
– Travel Theme

Summer Floral Style

Vintage Style

Classic

Save The Date

It's always prudent to send a Save The Date well in advance, especially if your wedding falls on a busy date in the year, or during summer holiday season. A Save The Date simply needs to state that you are getting married and on what date. This gives your guests a chance to block out that date in advance for you, in case any other events arise.

A Save The Date can be the first part of your themed wedding stationery, OR it can be a very simple thing like a basic card, an email or even a text.

If you are having a very clear theme for you wedding you might want to send something quirky.

Here are some other cool ideas to consider:

Stickers

Send a large sticker version of your wedding date to friends and family. This way they can stick it on their kitchen cupboard and easily remember the date!

You can print these at home using sticker sheets bought from the internet, just make sure your ink won't cost a fortune and that your printer is up to itThere are companies that will create stickers and other personalised items for you without you having to do any work at all, but this is a more costly option.

Jane from Cambridge:

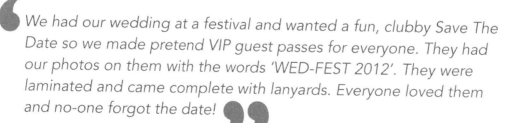

We had our wedding at a festival and wanted a fun, clubby Save The Date so we made pretend VIP guest passes for everyone. They had our photos on them with the words 'WED-FEST 2012'. They were laminated and came complete with lanyards. Everyone loved them and no-one forgot the date!

Fridge magnets

Another fun way to send your nuptials notice is by creating a fridge magnet. You can buy blank fridge magnets in bulk quite cheaply online. You'll need to print off your information and slot it into each blank magnet case. Or if you have the budget you can have these made for you as well.

E-cards

You can send a personalised e-card from sites such as **Jib Jab** or **Moonpig**. Some let you add you and your partner's faces to a funny card and can be sent in bulk out to friends and family.

Elizabeth from London:

Our wedding was going to be a surprise location so we sent out Save The Dates in the style of a ransom note, with individual letters cut out and stuck on a piece of paper which said 'IF YOU WANT TO SEE LIZ AND BRIAN GET MARRIED THEN SAVE THE DATE 31.3.13 !' It was so cheap and quick to do because we scanned one and made copies.

Weddings abroad

If you're getting married away from home why not send a Save The Date which hints at where the wedding will be located? For example if in Greece send a jar of olives with a specially personalised label; for Italy the same could go for a bottle of olive oil; for America how about a dollar bill?

Dan from Oxford:

My wife is Chinese and we were having an oriental themed event so we found a company on Ebay who made us personalised fortune cookies. When you cracked into them it said 'Confucius says Save The Date 14.09.13 – Sal and Dan'.

Beach weddings

Send a pebble with the names and date written on it in a pretty pen. Cheap to find on any beach (but a wbit more expensive to post!). Or send a message in a bottle, which is both romantic and mysterious.

Layout and Content

The layout choices of your invitations can vary from the very traditional wording to the more modern relaxed approach.

A typical Traditional Day Invitation layout:

Mr & Mrs William Smith request the pleasure of the company of

...

on the occasion of
the marriage of their daughter

Kelly Rose

to

Mr James Archie Jones

at All Saints Church Hove on Saturday 2nd May 2015
at 2 o'clock
and afterwards at Holingbury House, Hove

R.S.V.P.
256 Blatchington Road, Hove, East Sussex, BN3 by 5th November

Remember that ideally you should have three different guest lists; Daytime guests; Evening guests; Standby guests. Always send out the Daytime invites first then, once you start getting RSVPs back, you will be able to back fill any 'declines' with people from your Standby list.

Your evening invitations will need to have a less information on them but still keep within the theme of your daytime designs.

A typical Evening Invitation layout:

Mr & Mrs William Smith request the pleasure of the company of

....

at an Evening Reception to celebrate the marriage of their daughter

Kelly Rose

to

Mr James Archie Jones

to be held at Holingbury House, Hove
on Saturday 2nd May 2015 at 8 o'clock

R.S.V.P.

256 Blatchington Road, Hove, East Sussex, BN3 by 5th November

If you are taking a more modern approach and your guests are being invited by the bride and groom themselves, as opposed to by the bride's parents, then try the following:

Kelly & James Are Getting Hitched!

Please join us at :

All Saints Church Hove
on Saturday 2nd May 2015 at 2 o'clock
and afterwards at Holingbury House, Hove

R.S.V.P.
256 Blatchington Road, Hove, East Sussex, BN3 by 5th November

Making Your Own Invitations

If you're dead set on hand making your wedding stationery remember that it's not just one invite that you have to create, it's probably hundreds. Hand sewing tiny roses onto three hundred cards can soon become a huge chore, so the key is to make it a simple yet effective design.

Choose embellishments that come with adhesive already attached, ie sticky back ribbon, or 'peel off' shapes make life a lot easier.

Handmade cards can end up costing even more than store bought by the time you buy up half of Hobbycraft, so be sure to think carefully about just why you want to make them from scratch. If it's because you want to use your creativity and produce something personal and unique, then great. But if it's to save money then you might want to follow these useful tips:

All of the cool designs featured on previous pages are actually vectors from a stock photo site called **Shutterstock** (www.shutterstock.com). If you or a friend are budding graphic designers or handy with a computer, these templates are fairly simple to tweak – just pick a design you love, download for a few pounds, then add in your own names and text on top of the cool design, ready for you to have printed. This can be much cheaper than hiring a designer to make them from scratch – and there are hundreds of designs to choose from!

1. Avoid buying your products from big stores or retailers. They will charge a lot more than markets or on-line shops.

2. If buying in bulk, always buy a small quantity first to test the product. You don't want to be left with 1000 fluorescent orange rose buds.

3. Allow time. The cheapest deals on embellishments and beads, etc. will be from the States and China but they will usually take 3-4 weeks to arrive. Build this into your timeline.

4. Check stock levels. If you're buying pink polka dot ribbon from a store check how much they have or if they can get more of the same colour/design. The last thing you need is to run out and then have to start all over again.

5. Don't buy card stock that's pre-scored. You can get 200 sheets of A4 card from Poundland for the princely sum of £1. When folded it makes the perfect A5 sized card, you just need to score each sheet down the middle before folding. So that's 200 invites for just £1. And they sell envelopes too!

6. Check how much it's going to cost for you to print bulk items from your printer. A colour cartridge can cost up to £30 and might only print 50 good sheets. If it's going to cost you £180 in ink you might want to think about using a local printer.

Apps and Websites

A really cost effective way (it's free!) of creating an invitation is by creating your very own App. It's simple to do but can be time consuming, depending on how many photos and additional content you require. It also relies on your guests being computer savvy and having a smart phone or tablet to download the App on to.

Simply search on the internet 'I want to build an App' and a whole host of websites will appear. **www.theappbuilder.com** is an easy one to navigate. You just cut and paste your information into the pages, using one of the templates they provide. When it's finished you have the option of publishing it for free or paying a fee to publish. The only difference being that if you publish for free they include a link to their site, which is very subtle. Then you email a link out to all of your guests and they can instantly download it from there! It's a dynamic platform so you can update or add items at any time. It even provides links to stores you have wedding lists at. How cool is that?

Another useful resource is a wedding website which details pretty much of all the same types of items you might have in the App, but that is accessible to all people on the internet, not just smart phone and tablet owners.

This can be great for showing your guests the venue and live maps on how to get there. It can detail accommodation available with links to individual sites for easy booking. This will save you having to print and send them all this info with the invitation.

You can even have a message board so you can leave notes for people to see or use as a tool for your guests to get in touch regarding lift shares or other transport details.Afterwards you can share photographs and videos of the big day with people who couldn't attend, as well as your memories from your honeymoon.

> *www.weddingpath.co.uk*
> *www.momentville.com*
> *www.gettingmarried.co.uk*
> *www.2haveand2hold.com*
> *www.mywedding.com*

Seating Plans and Table Stationery

You will need a table number or name on each of your banquet tables inside the main room. The venue may provide you with numbers already but it's always nice to have personalised ones to continue your theme.

You may not have an overarching colour theme or motif that you want to incorporate into your table designs and seating plan, and wish to simply use an elegant black and white table number to identify them with. But if you do have a theme then why not extend that design to the table, like the example of a movie themed wedding below.

Cute picture frames or mini chalk-boards are also a lovely idea!

Great idea for a movie themed wedding – a mini clapperboard!

At the entrance to the main banquet hall it's usual to have a Seating Plan chart – guests look for their name to discover which table they are on.

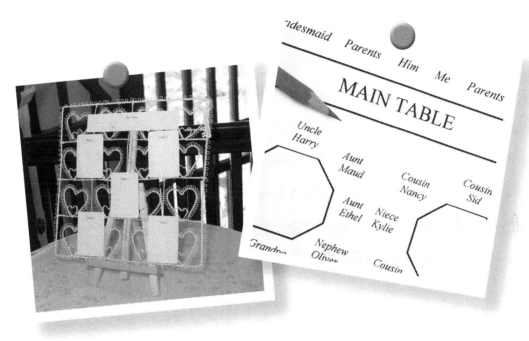

Here are some other ideas of how to display your seating plan:

Vintage Wedding

Take a vintage looking suitcase, preferably an old leather one, and have it sitting opened up. In the lid and base you can fit your table plan with the lists of where everyone is siting. It looks especially good if you line the suitcase with a floral or lace paper for a truly old-school feel.

3D Board

Quite a popular theme is birds and bird cages. You can buy quite large birdcage shaped memo boards which are actually 3D metal cages. They have pegs on them so you could use this as your board and peg the table information onto it.

Casino theme

Each guest is sent a playing card with their invitation and asked to bring it with them to the wedding. They then sit at the table which is named after their card. You can buy giant playing cards to use as the table markers, for little money from most party shops or on-line.

Tips for Table Names

Table names don't even have to have anything to do with your colour theme or wedding design, they can just be linked to something you and your partner love to love!

Musicians

Why not name tables after musicians that you think your guests reflect? Put Grandma Rose on the Mozart table and Cousin Billy on the ACDC table.

Poems

Each table can be named after a poet with one of their most famous works rolled in a scroll at each place setting. This could also be the wedding favour.

Cities

Pick cities around the globe that mean a lot to you and your guests; for instance where you first met, your first holiday, your honeymoon destination or your home towns. Or if you are planning to honeymoon in NYC, then table names like Central Park, Broadway, Times Square and Fifth Avenue would be cool!

Name Place Cards

The best brides and grooms consider carefully who they will seat next to whom. It's a strategic task that can forge friendships, love, future marriages, and best of all avoid family feuds erupting! You can have your place cards match the theme of your other stationery or the name place could be shown by using a decoration that they could keep afterwards.

Name tag is attached to a cute wedding favour at each place setting.

Hand-written names on driftwood at a beach wedding

Order of Service

Whether you're having a civil or religious ceremony, handing out an order of service to your guests as they arrive will ensure everyone knows what to expect and doesn't sneak off at a crucial moment (ie when you're exchanging your vows!). Some people like to include the complete breakdown of the service – including the words of the minister and the response of the couple – whereas others use it only as a guide with the basic details of the service and perhaps printed words to the hymns or songs too.

You might be unfamiliar with the wedding service and uncertain as to the wording of an order of service. Ask the person carrying out the service/ceremony how they would like the information to be presented and run it past them before going to print.

Here is an example of a traditional order of service:

The Marriage of

Mary Jane Smith
to
Mr. David Jones

St. Mary's Church, Oxford,
Saturday 2nd July 2007

BRIDAL MARCH "Lohengrin" ~ Wagner

HYMN
Enter words for 1st hymn here

THE MARRIAGE
Conducted by Reverend Peter Brown
Signing of the Register

READING
Enter reading details here

HYMN
Enter words for 2nd Hymn here

PRAYERS
WEDDING MARCH ~ Mendelssohn

You might prefer a more informal style, especially if you are having a non-religious ceremony, without hymns or prayers. This tends to be referred to more as a wedding programme, or Order of The Day, and it can detail the whole days events. Great if you have a lot of entertainment in the evenings or in different locations around the venue.

Guest Book

Most weddings feature a guest book so that people can leave their messages for the happy couple. Alternatively you could have a memo board or tree branches with pegs – people can write little notes on cards and pin them up throughout the day!

Photobooths

Hiring a photo-booth is currently a very popular thing for weddings and parties. Provide guests with fun props and they can take amazing pics on the day, and glue them into your guest book along with their message. This will give you an amazing and fun guest book to look back at in years to come.

Thank You Cards

If you're very lucky you'll get tons of lovely gifts from your guests, so don't forget to plan a marathon thank you card writing session on your return from honeymoon.

People take a lot of time and money buying just the right gift for a wedding and it's only polite and courteous to let them know that you received it and are grateful for it.

You can use simple store bought cards if you want to keep costs and time to a minimum. But it won't take much to continue your theme and really impress them by matching your thank you cards to all of your other stationery as well.

Another lovely idea is to take a photo, or a selfie, of the pair of you holding, or using the item you were given in a fun way. Print this on card or photo paper and write a short personal '*We LOVE our toaster, thank you so much*' on the back. Much more personal than a standard card, and less to write!

Venues

Do you dream of a lavish hotel reception with crisp white tablecloths and a 4 course silver-served meal? Or would you be just as happy having a right old knees-up and fish & chips at the local pub? Or perhaps something in between?

The venue usually creates the biggest dent in your budget so you need get this right and make sure you get the maximum bang for your buck. Make sure you know how many guests you need to cater for before venturing out into the world of venues as most places base their costs 'per head'. So know your numbers and what your budget is. There's no point going to see The Savoy if all you can afford is the working men's club!

There are an amazing selection of venues around the UK that offer Wedding packages, most of whom can cater for your ceremony requirements as well, if you decide against a separate church service. So, once you've established a budget, the next big question is location, location, location. Can your guests get there ok? Is there enough room to accommodate everyone? And if you're choosing a country house hotel or venue that is fairly rural – is there enough accommodation nearby for all your guests to stay over, and is it affordable enough for every price bracket. Weddings can be hugely expensive for guests to attend, so if the only accommodation on offer is a £250 per night room at the venue hotel, don't be surprised if some of your guest list can't make it.

If you are having a church or registry office wedding then you will probably already have an idea of the area you wish to be looking at. You will want it to be either walking distance, have sufficient parking at both venues so that guests can get from one to another, OR lay on transport yourself (which is another cost to consider). Just make sure that routes between locations are simple to navigate. You don't want half the wedding party lost somewhere on the A605. Also avoid routes which take guests onto motorways. One bad traffic jam could mess up the whole day.

Hotels and fit for purpose wedding venues

These types of venue should be the most organised for your type of event. They are well versed in the wedding biz and will most likely host at least three receptions a week in peak season.

If you want a hassle-free, complete wedding package then this type of venue is probably best for you as they will be able to organise everything from the ceremony and flowers to catering and accommodation.

Of course you don't have to use all of their services and it's important to find out what they can offer in their packages and what is additional. Make sure you ask all of the right questions before signing on the dotted line because often a presumed expense won't be included. There can be a lot of hidden extras which you need to be aware of so check your contract thoroughly and ask questions like this:

- Does the price include VAT? (if not, add 20%)
- Are there any extra staff costs and is service included?
- What exactly does the cost per guest include?
- How much is corkage if you bring your own fizz or wine?
- Is the cloakroom free?
- Are there extra costs for lighting/power?
- Can they accommodate your band/dj/entertainment?
- Is there a marquee hire charge?
- Is there an extra charge for tables, crockery, glasses, linen or chairs?
- Will you get exclusive use or are there other weddings there on the same day?
- If it's a hotel, do they give reduced room rates for guests?
- How many staff will be on the main bar during your event?

Not everyone is comfortable with negotiating and you may wish to simply take a straight package deal. But most venues will offer discounts, or at least throw in a few extras, if you just ask the right questions. Always do this before you sign a contract though, see just how much you can convince them to add in, whether it's chair covers, champagne or after dinner mints!

Off-Peak

Much like the 10.45 from Brighton to London, Weddings venues have their 'off peak' times. Meaning that if you pick a less popular day, like a Friday or Sunday, it can cut the cost of the reception venue by up to half, and Monday to Thursday could be even less.

The flip side of that is that fewer guests may be able to attend if you pick a weekday, but it's something to consider if you a) are on a tight budget or b) you really want to keep numbers down.

You can also save money by booking a winter wedding as venues tend to have less bookings during this period. Packages are usually reduced by up to 60% of the summer price. Plus planning for a winter wedding means the venue is likely to already be dressed for Christmas so even more of a saving there!

Time will be precious for you and whilst it's a lovely thing to be out and about visiting locations it also takes time and money, so try to shortlist your favourite five venues before making appointments to visit them.

You want to make totally sure you've chosen the right venue for you, so take this checklist along so you can tick everything off.

It is licensed to carry out a civil ceremony should you choose to have one there?	
What is the maximum capacity for the ceremony and reception?	
Will you have use of a garden, or is there somewhere you could erect a marquee to make more space for evening guests?	
Is there a private room you could use to touch up your make-up/take a breather? And is there a room the bridesmaids could use? Will this cost any extra?	
How many toilets are available for use?	
Who will be your point of contact on the day and will they be available at all times to help with any problems?	
Is it licensed to sell alcohol?	
Is there a covered smoking area?	
Does it have a late license? If so, what is the latest the reception can end?	
Are you allowed to use your own caterers, put up decorations and source the flowers form an outside company or do you have to use their suppliers?	
Do they have any arrangements with suppliers, DJs, hotels or taxi firms who may give you a discount?	
Can you access the venue the day before the wedding? If not, what time will people be allowed in on the big day to check that everything is as planned?	
Do they have a cake stand and /or cake table?	
Do they have a PA system for speeches and a projector in case you want to display photos?	
Do they have a music system so you can play your own songs through an MP3 player should you want to? Are there any noise restrictions?	
Is there a secure area where you could store your gifts?	
Do they allow confetti?	
Do they allow candles and will someone ensure they're changed once they're burnt down?	
Do they have a toastmaster you could use?	
Is there a separate bar area where evening guests can wait if the wedding breakfast runs over?	
How many bar staff will be on duty- weddings can be spoiled by long waits for drinks!	
What parking facilities do they have?	

Gardens and Marquee

Garden parties can be amazing in summer, so if you have a family or a friend with a sizeable garden, ask if they'd consider allowing you to use it for your wedding. As weather can be very unreliable, you should definitely use a marquee. The average size for a wedding reception to seat 100 would be about 10 x 20 metres.

There's lots to plan for this type of event, especially if you're doing it from scratch, but if you're using an events company or a caterers then they should be able to help take the
pressure off of you.

The main items to consider:

- **Catering** Hot or cold? Will there be cooking facilities? You may have to hire an additional tent to add to the side of the marquee to act as a kitchen area. Caterers normally provide their own mobile equipment but check if they also have their own tent.

- **Toilets** Portaloos are so last year. Get yourself a nice set of luxury toilets and dress them up with ribbons and flowers and posh soaps. If possible have a disabled sized loo as part of the arrangement because Brides are unlikely to be able to squeeze into a normal sized portable toilet cubicle in their beautiful dress.

- **Dance floor** Don't leave your marquee without a hard floor unless you're having a festival theme and everyone is going to rock up wearing wellies. There's nothing worse than satin stilettos stuck in mud!

- **Electrics** If you're having a candlelight and acoustic affair then this won't be an issue, but if your band, DJ or bar requires power then you may need to consider hiring a generator. Plus how else will you plug in all of those pretty fairy lights?

- **Furniture** You'll need to hire not only the chair covers but the chairs and tables as well. The average price for a banquet chair is about £3.50 per chair. Tables cost approximately £15 each. Remember though that price is per piece, per day. Most companies will let you keep the items until Monday from a Saturday hire at no extra cost, but make sure you ask the question when getting quotes. Is delivery, collection and VAT also included in the price?

- **Heating** Even warm summer days can bring cool evenings and so you'll need to have outdoor heaters on standby especially if your event falls in the winter months. These can eat electricity so if you're using a friend's home location make sure you've warned them of the impending charges.

- **Parking** If the location you're using has a field for parking just make sure it's clear of animals – and the things they might leave behind. Also ensure if there's a chance of rain that cars are going to be able to get out of the field if it gets muddy. If it's in a more built up area speak to neighbours to let them know that traffic will be busy. They may even offer to let you use their driveways.

Holiday Rental Property

Holiday rentals can make fantastic wedding venues and often provide a five-star venue for two-star prices, with the added bonus of accommodation for your guests.

For example a 10 bedroom luxury chateau in France which sleeps 22 can cost £5,000 for a week's rental. If you consider that 10 double rooms at a luxury hotel for a week would likely cost upwards of £10,000, it suddenly seems like the bargain of the year!

But you do usually need to sort your own caterers, table hire and lighting, etc. so do your sums first. The advantage is that it becomes your house for the week (or weekend), so there's no corkage charge and no fixed menus to stick to.

You'll need to ask the owner to check that they are happy to use it as a venue before throwing a bash there. They may charge extra, but they'll often help you with local contacts for things like catering and music.

Pubs, village halls and other venues

If you prefer a more low key affair then using a pub function room or a village hall can be a great location and at a fraction of the cost of big hotels.

You still need to book ahead if it's a busy month because at the average hire cost of £100 per night for the whole place, these gets booked up early.

If there isn't a bar in the venue then you need to ask them about licensing – do they have a license for alcohol and what are the stipulations regarding this? Can you bring in your own mobile bar person or even your own alcohol?

Also find out when you have to have it cleared up by. If they've got it booked the next day you might have to have everything out the same night as the wedding reception or very early the next morning. Do you have friends that will be willing to do this for you?

Food &
Drink

Welcome Drinks

Once your guests have arrived at the reception they will be ready for a drink and and a mingle so it's nice to provide them with a little glass of something special whilst you are getting 'papped' by the wedding photographer.

Glasses should be poured and ready to serve as soon as the guests arrive and a choice of two or three (one being non-alcoholic) drinks is what would normally be expected.

Drinks can vary depending on the time of year. For a winter wedding it would be fun to serve something like eggnog, mulled wine or hot chocolate.

Popular welcome drinks:

Champagne
Cava/Prosecco
Buck's Fizz (use sparkling wine and not champagne to save cash)
Pimms
Orange juice
Elderflower presse

Canapés

These are an added luxury which won't always be in budget but if you can afford them your guests will be over the moon. You can guarantee they'll be hungry by the time they arrive at the reception, and it's always better to serve less drink and a few canapés then have a bunch of sozzled guests on your hands! I've been to so many weddings where the guests are absolutely starving as they haven't eaten since 8am, and spend 2-3 hours drinking in between the ceremony and the meal, dreaming of food!

The Wedding Breakfast

The wedding 'breakfast' is an old-fashioned term for the reception meal. In the 18th and 19th centuries it was only legal to get married before noon in England, hence the term for the meal afterwards.

This part of the day usually takes up quite a large portion of your budget so choose wisely and ensure that you get exactly what you and your partner want. It's nice to cater for all tastes but remember that it's your day and you should choose something that you really love to eat and drink.

First of all pick a venue which suits your catering needs. If you want to bring in third party caterers, that may rule out a large number of locations as most hotels require you to use their catering team.

Budget-wise, self-catering can be a lot cheaper but you'd probably be best to stick to a buffet or barbecue. Table service for 100 guests is a big ask of any friend or relative, unless of course they are a professional caterer.

Whether you choose to cater for yourselves or let your venue take care of it all you'll still have some decisions to make regarding the formality of your wedding breakfast.

Hotel Catering

Most hotels will offer you a package meeting most of the traditional wedding requirements such as:

Welcome drink
Welcome canapés
Three course meal
Table wine
Table water
Toasting champagne
Evening buffet

The price is usually per head and they will have different menu choices for different price packages. You will often be invited to a tasting evening at the venue where you and your partner can sample smaller versions of the choices on offer.

A lot of venues will allow you to supply your own wine or champagne but they will charge you what is called 'corkage'. This is a fee per bottle which can sometimes outweigh the benefit of BYO (bring your own). The average hotel charges £15 per bottle for their house red and £14 corkage on any wine you might bring. So this is often only beneficial if you want to provide a much more expensive selection of wines, otherwise you may as well plump for the house plonk.

If you've decided to plan and provide your own food and drink then there are a multitude of menu options available.

Buffet

A hot or cold a buffet is always a big hit because you can cater to all tastes and appetites, but you'd do well to avoid sandwiches if the food it going to be sitting around because these dry out very quickly.

BBQ

Alongside the cold selections above you could have a barbecue for your guests serving a range of posh burgers and sausages plus veggie options like grilled halloumi and vegetable patties. Add to this a table of delicious salads and side dishes and you can feed your guests well on a limited budget. This is a great choice if you're having a garden party or your venue has a lovely outdoor space.

Top Tip

Ask your venue if they can provide a BBQ instead of a formal meal – most venues have that option, especially during the summer months.

Hog Roast

You can hire a hog roast relatively cheaply and it's a great idea for both the main reception or the evening buffet. There are companies that specialise in this. Served in bread rolls it makes a fantastic late night snack for slightly tipsy, hungry guests! Alternatively, ask the venue if they can do bacon rolls (instead of a buffet) late in the evening. There's nothing like a tray of hot, delicious bacon rolls appearing at 11pm when guests are weary from the dancefloor!

Afternoon Tea

If you are going to be arriving at the reception for about 3.30-4pm you might fancy hosting an Afternoon Tea instead of a standard meal plan.

Serve everything to the table, that way everything will be nice and fresh for your guests. If you can, use tiered plates and vintage style cake stands to really give a 'Palm Court' feel to the occasion.

Afternoon tea offers you lots of fun dressing ideas for your tables too. Why not use old crockery for the centre pieces? Or teapots with fresh flowers sprouting from their lid and spout? If shabby chic is your thing then this is perfect because doilies and lace looks very ladylike when accompanied by china cups and saucers. Just make sure the food offered is substantial enough and there's plenty on offer – a couple of cucumber crustless sandwiches per head just won't fill your hungry guests!

Food with a Theme

A wonderful way to tie your whole wedding theme together is with a specially selected menu for the occasion.

If it's a Hollywood affair then why not put popcorn chicken on the menu with red carpet cheesecake? For a Great Gatsby inspired 'do' you could simply serve cocktails and canapés, and a dessert served in a martini glass would really fizz!

If you've a partner from another country then you may already be contemplating an exotic cuisines like Chinese, Indian or Moroccan, which are a break from the norm but make an exciting change.

Fish and chips are always a success at any party and you can have your very own fish and chip van to deliver the food straight to your guests. Great for a seaside wedding!

Desserts

Want to save £££? Then why not serve your wedding cake as the dessert. So often the cake doesn't get eaten because everyone is so full. Perhaps you won't have a standard fruit cake for this very reason. A giant jelly and sweet cake or a tower of profiteroles could be just what the people want for their pudding.

If you can't decide on one sweet option a popular choice is to have a mini cake buffet. This is wonderful because it caters for all tastes. Think miniature versions of your favourite dishes like mini cheesecake, mini cream cakes, mini banoffee pies, meringues, chocolate sundaes etc. Budget for at least 3 per guest as they're bound to be very popular!

Your Wedding Cake

The wedding cake normally plays a key part in your day, and should even have its own listing on the Order of The Day. The cutting of the cake symbolises the cementing of an intimate bond between you and your loved one.

There are many options available to you and lots of decisions to be made. Will you have a sponge cake or fruit cake? How many tiers would you like? What decorations should you choose? Should it even be a cake at all? Don't be overwhelmed by all of the choices. This is one of the fun decisions and you need to embrace the tasting process with open arms.

A traditional wedding cake is made from sponge or fruit cake, has three tiers and is iced with a thick white royal icing. On average it feeds about 100 guests. But there are plenty of twists on the original design and the best way to find out what you like is to try them all! If you can't choose then why not have a different flavour for each tier? You could even have the top level made as a fruit cake which you can then freeze and save for a milestone anniversary. If you do decide to do that it's to have a high alcohol content in the fruitcake to keep it moist.

If a bakery or local cake company is creating your cake for you then book yourselves a tasting session. The best ones get booked up quickly for wedding season, up to a year in advance. So act quickly if you have your heart set on a custom design by a great cake company! You will usually visit them for a consultation and tasting session, agree and sign off on the design, and pay a deposit to hold your date. You will then pay the balance a few weeks before the big day. Most cake companies will deliver and set up the cake, and hire you any stands or accessories you may need.

The Alternative Touch

If you don't fancy the idea of a traditional cake – or the idea of spending hundreds of pounds one it – and want something a bit different there are loads of other options available.

Macaroon Tower

These little French meringue morsels have really become de rigour with the fashion set over the last few years. Therefore if you want a cutting edge, on-trend wedding cake why not go for a tower of pretty coloured macaroons?

Macaroon Tower

Cheesecake

No, not the sweet biscuity type, we're talking real cheese! This is always a huge hit with the guests. You simply buy rounds of cheese in varying sizes; Stilton; cheddar; Camembert; Wensleydale; Brie. Stack them one on top of the other and decorate with grapes, flowers and the topper of your choice.

Jelly Tower

A fun one for the kids and those adults that just won't grow up. Tiers of jelly served with fresh fruit and cream is a great option if you're not having a dessert as well. It's always fun to add a little vodka to the jelly mix, though be careful kids don't get their hands on it!

Cupcakes

Always a favourite and really easy to make in advance. You can buy cupcake tower stands quite inexpensively from your local craft shop, or even cheaper on Ebay. Decorate the cupcakes to suit your colour scheme. You could also combine a cupcake tower with a one-layer matching cake – that way you get to 'cut the cake' but also have a cupcake per gusts to enjoy.

Store bought

Sticking to the cake theme you can buy pre-made, pre-iced wedding cakes from supermarkets like Marks and Spencer's and Sainsbury's. If you can't afford a wedding cake designer then why not go halfway and have someone decorate a store bought one for you? Your guests will never know the difference!

Your Wedding Dress

The most exciting decision for any bride is what gown they will wear on their big day. Some people will have a vague idea of what they like, whilst others will have absolutely none. Either way you can pretty much bet your bottom dollar that the style you think you like will be the polar opposite of what you end up purchasing!

Wedding dresses come in a vast range of prices – from as low as £85 right up to tens of thousands of pounds. Whilst you do need a rough idea of what your budget is, it's always fun to try on all price points because a dress that you fall in love with which is out of your price bracket can always be replicated by a dressmaker for a fraction of the cost.

To start your search scour wedding magazines for pieces that inspire you. Cut them out and add to a scrapbook that you can take to different stores with you. If you show shop owners a dress you like they will more than likely have something similar in stock that they can identify quickly.

Not au fait with all the wedding dress lingo? Here's the lowdown on the luxury fabrics you'll come across:

Duchess Satin

This is a very heavy satin, very luxurious and quite expensive. You can feel the quality of a dress made from this fabric but be warned its weight makes it unsuitable for wearing on hot days or in warm climates. Like the wicked witch of the west you will literally melt.

Lace

A cheap lace will have you look like a giant net curtain, a good quality material will give an elegant, vintage feel. Think Princess Kate. You want to avoid an entire dress of lace, unless you're going for a 1950's look and it works best as an overlay to other materials. You'll see a lot of dresses with sheer lace arms, which tend to suit ladies with slender arms.

Chiffon

A true chiffon is made of silk but there are many synthetic forms of the fabric which look just as good. They are just a little warmer to wear because of the material content. Chiffon is a free flowing, sheer silky material. It caresses the form and works very well when cut on the bias, which is when the fabric is cut diagonally not straight, meaning it can have more movement.

Silk Georgette

Much like chiffon this is a light, floaty material used mainly as a top layer to a wedding dress. It makes a beautiful train from the shoulders and reacts in a gorgeous manner when there's a light breeze in the air.

You'll also want to cram up on your dress shapes and designs before you venture to a wedding store because otherwise it can seem like they are speaking a foreign language.

Here's a list of styles that you're likely to come across on your travels:

Fishtail

This design cinches the waist and hugs the hips before spilling out into a beautiful 'fish' tail at the base of the dress. It often has a strapless bodice (top) and embroidery or beading on the tail and bust area. This shape is very evocative of Hollywood and even now each year you will see many fishtail dresses on the red carpet at the Oscars. It suits a curvy figure with the big three B's – bountiful hips, boobs and bottom!

A-Line

The most adaptable design for any figure this dress shape had a fitted bodice, cinched waist and then the skirt flows out from the waist to create an A shape to the floor or knee. You'll find hundreds if dresses in this design and it is a really good option for most body shapes.

Princess

The meringue, as it has been come to be known, is probably every little girl's idea of what a wedding dress looks like. Think Disney princess and you get the picture. It generally has a sweetheart shaped bodice, a cinched waist and then an explosion of fabric from the waist down.

Straight

Very Pre-Raphaelite in design, a straight cut dress suits small busted, small hipped ladies. It's one piece of fabric straight the way down with minimal darts or waistbands. Think of a long 1920's flapper dress and you'll get the idea.

Two piece dresses

If you have a bigger bottom than bust or vice versa then this style of dress will suit you very well. It can still look like a one piece but the bodice and skirt are made separately, meaning you can even order different sizes for each part. A two piece dress was traditionally for a second marriage and looked more like a smart suit in days gone by, but this has all changed and separates have been firmly embraced by the 21st century.

Where To Buy Your Dress

There are a huge selection of places to buy that special gown – from the high end designer boutique to the high street store. Budget may limit your options for the final piece, but not the final design because there are so many styles available for every price range.

The Bridal Store

An afternoon spent at a Bridal store with your Mum or bridesmaids is a truly beautiful experience. The very posh ones will sometimes serve you and your guests fizz and nibbles or cakes, which makes it all the more special. And why not? It's a milestone experience and you should savour every moment.

Most bridal shops require you to make an appointment in advance as this ensures you have an assistant and changing room set aside for you. If you're super organised email them some photos of dress styles you're interested in. That way they can have some ready for you to look at as soon as you arrive. Many stores even charge a fee for these appointments, probably to put off time wasters and cover the costs of any fizz or nibbles they provide!

Most bridal designers will have their range available at only a small selection of approved stores – so if you have your heart set on something by a particular designer, or even a specific dress you saw in a magazine in mind, then you need to check their website and find the stockist near you. Ready to wear gowns form designers can still take up to nine months to be finished because even though the designs are not exclusive, the garments are still all made to order.

For anything bespoke – both designed and made just for you – you normally have to order directly from the designer and this is understandably a far more expensive option than the ready to wear collections. For a bespoke gown you need to be ordering at least one year in advance.

Bridal stores offer the complete package from gowns, veils and tiaras to outfits for mother of the bride and bridesmaids too. The assistants will be able to advise you on the sizes, fit and colouring of the dresses and what suits your physique. But take along an honest friend or family member as well because you need someone to tell you how it is, rather than just 'coo' – although that is rather nice sometimes!

When purchasing from a bridal store you can book as many fittings as you wish. However be aware that they will probably charge you about £150 for each visit, depending on whether it includes bridesmaids as well. Many bridal shops won't allow you to take any photos until you have actually paid your deposit. This is probably so that brides cannot take photos of gowns which they will then take away to a dressmaker to replicate!

Finally, when you order your gown from a bridal shop, it's important to check the contract (your dress will have one). Read it carefully to ensure you don't end up with the wrong size or colour, and make sure to get every detail – the designer, style number, measurements, delivery date, the price of the gown and number of fittings included as well as the deposit amount – all in writing.

High street

There are more and more high street stores stocking wedding dresses and the standard of design and quality of materials are surprisingly good.

Big department stores even have their own bridal dressing rooms which you can book appointments for, just like a bridal store.

There are a lot of famous designers working with these big shops, such the Designers for Debenhams range, and BHS, Monsoon and Coast are well know for their great, affordable wedding ranges.. Top designer power for a fraction of the cost? Amazing!

These dresses are what's known as 'off the peg', in that you can but the exact one you try on and take home that day. But most stores employ either an in-house seamstress or can recommend a local one to help with any alterations that might need to be done.

The high street is also ideal for bridesmaids dresses – splurge the budget on your own custom dress, then make savings by buying gorgeous off-the-peg bridesmaids dresses!

Discount or outlet dresses

If you fancy getting your hands on a cut price Vera Wang or Temperley it's really not all that difficult. Your first port of call is the sales, and a lot of designers will have a sample sale at least once a year.

If you're dedicated (and have the money) it's worth a strategic trip to New York. Places like Wang have incredible sample sales twice a year. It's a bit of a scrum but with a bit of perseverance you'll get yourself a true bargain. The saving alone will probably cover your travel costs. So start looking well in advance to ensure you don't miss these annual dates!

Flying abroad may seem pretty extreme, and only for those who still want to shell out some pretty major money. Those who'd like a bit of designer love on a more demure budget can head to Bicester Village designer outlet in Oxfordshire. There are loads of fabulous designer stores offering amazing discounts. It doesn't have a dedicated bridal store but you'll find Temperley, DVF, Ralph Lauren and Gucci to name but a few. And there are always wedding dresses tucked away in stock rooms. If you don't see them make sure you ask the assistants. You can even get your bridal lingerie there as they boast La Perla and Agent Provocateur outlets too.

Vintage

If you're planning to wear your mum's or your gran's dress, make sure you check the fabric thoroughly before attempting to try it on. Aged fabrics can be very delicate things and the last thing you want is to tear the seams.

Once you're happy that it's workable, take it to a seamstress and have her fit it to your body shape. If it's too small don't worry because a good seamstress can add panels and embellishments to alter the garment to suit your needs.

Vintage stores will sometimes have the most gorgeous gowns and the same rules apply. The beauty of recycling a vintage dress is that it's likely to be unique and unusual. You can also add extra details to bring it up to date if you wish.

Use a dressmaker

If you have your heart set on either a major designer gown or a unique one-off piece of your own design then you need to find a great dress maker. There are some really talented seamstresses out there waiting to help you create your dream wedding dress.

Take lots of photos with you and any sketches of ideas that you have had. You might even have pattern for them to follow – Vogue sell a large selection of wedding dress patterns, available in stores like John Lewis or easily found online.

Just as with a bridal store, ensure that you agree the amount of fittings, cost and timescale in writing before handing over any money. It's normal to pay half the cost at the time of ordering and half on completion, but this does vary from person to person.

There are plenty of overseas offers on platforms like Ebay, with a lot of dressmakers in the Far East offering designer copies for just a few hundred pounds. The downside to this type of order is that you can't see a sample prior to ordering and so you take your chances with the sizing, materials and colours. But if they have a good amount of reviews then at those low prices it can be worth the gamble.

Be mindful of this bride's story though...

I desperately wanted to buy an Ian Stewart dress, having seen them in celebrity magazines, but they were way out of my price range. I saw a company on Ebay in China selling copies for a couple of hundred pounds so I ordered a beautiful design in rose pink but when it arrived it was a lurid hot pink colour and the material was scratchy and uncomfortable. I tried to return it but the cost to post it back was too much. I ended up getting a real Ian Stewart dress from a second hand wedding dress shop in the end. It was expensive but at least half of the original price and worth every penny to me on the day!

Tips when trying on dresses:

- Take a selection of bras with you to try on with your dresses
- Take a pair of heels the height you will feel comfortable to wear on the day
- If you like one designer's dress, but the neckline or embellishments are not to your liking, ask the assistants if the designer makes something else similar, which is quite often the case.
- Don't be put off if the dress is too big. Ask the assistants for clips to help you visualise it in the right size.
- Try the same dress in every shade it comes in. You might be surprised at what you find you like.
- Don't buy the first dress you try on, even if they offer you a discount and tell you it's the last one. It won't be. It's always best to wait two or three visits before you commit.

To hire or not to hire?

Needless to say if you do hire something you won't have something to pass down to future generations, but with styles changing so frequently these days I doubt that this is high on your list of priorities.

Things to consider when thinking when hiring wedding attire:

- The advantage of hiring is that you can have the latest designer dress at a fraction of the cost. Remember that you will have to take it back after the big day so you'll need to be really careful that nothing gets spilled on it.

- If you're heading straight off on honeymoon you'll need to trust someone to return it for you as soon as possible.

- The norm is for a gentleman to hire a morning suit because there is so little variation with them, and of course it can be personalized to fit in with the wedding theme using pocket squares and buttonholes.

- Hiring can be expensive so you may want to shop around for something second hand instead as it could work out costing the same – or even less – to buy.

Choosing a veil

A bride's veil is second only to her dress!

Obviously one of the most important factors in choosing a veil is that it compliments your dresses style and shape and emphasizes the focal points of your gown.

If you have an understated dress you can go for a more elaborate veil, and likewise if you have a very detailed dress it's best to go for something quite simple.

If you have a particular section of your dress you want to show off – maybe you have some detailing on the back or front panel? – you can select a veil that stops just before the focal point so it accentuates it. Alternatively you could choose something sheer so the detailing can still be clearly seen through it.

What length is best?

Fascinator veil

These are a modern twist on a 30's concept. They work particularly well if you have a high-necked gown, or you want to show off your dress in its entirety. It also adds a cool retro feel.

Shoulder length veil

Again, if you're keen to show off the whole of your dress you can go for something that rests on your shoulders. Generally these are around 20 inches long and work best with a modern style of gown.

Mid-length veil

These should fall halfway down your arm and they work well with princess dresses as the fullness emulates the romantic feel of the skirt.

Fingertip veils

These are usually around 35 inches and suit most dress shapes, although they are best avoided with princess dresses. More intricate veils of this length look lovely when worn with a simple, contemporary gown.

Knee length

This style of veil is around 45-50 inches and often features tiers. Again, they look lovely with simple contemporary dresses, but they also suit fuller gowns as they create a waterfall effect.

Ballet length veil

These fall just above the floor and suit full length column dresses. Lace patterns look stunning when paired with a fuss free dress, while plainer versions compliment more detailed gowns.

Chapel length

These veils are around 90 inches long and fall gently onto the floor. They are usually paired with dresses that have a train and are best avoided with dresses that are shorter than mind-calf.

Cathedral length

These veils are the most traditional. They drape along the floor and are generally around 120 inches long. They work best with full length, floaty gowns.

Hair & Make-up

Always choose your dress first before you decide how you are going to have your hair because your hairstyle needs to complement the style of the dress. Your dress determines how fancy or simple the hair style needs to be.

A fancy, detailed dress often lends itself towards a more simple, classic hair style. In reverse a simple dress design allows for more elaborate hair styles. If the dress has straps or a halter-neck, your hair will look gorgeous in an up-do, to keep the focus on your neckline.

Top Tip

Take pictures of practice styles. What we see in the mirror is often different to what we see in a picture and remember pictures are taken mostly from the front on the day. If all the detail is all at the back you won't get to see it!

- When you're booking your hair or make-up trials, why not try to make it for a day when you are going somewhere special like someone else's wedding, your hen night or a party?

- Have your colour and a trim done a week before the wedding. Try not to make any drastic changes to either the colour or the style that you may regret on the day.

- Wash and blow-dry your hair the night before the wedding. Never wash it on the day as it will be too soft to hold the style – most stylists prefer 1 or 2 days old hair to work on!

- Treat yourself to a spa day or treatments at a local salon a few days before the wedding. Have a facial, manicure, pedicure and any waxing done in the sanctuary of a stress -free environment.

- Do not put any fake tan on the day of the wedding. If you have to use fake make sure it's done professionally and several days before the big day.

- If you are on a tight budget, visit your salon on the morning of the wedding – it's cheaper than having someone come to you!

- Likewise, if you plan to do your own make-up, book a session with the likes of Mac or Bobbi Brown. Photograph the results you love, and ask for a list of the products and shades used so that you can recreate this look yourself on the day.

- If you don't' usually wear much make-up, you may feel overly made-up when done by a professional. Bear in mind, though, that on camera this may look a lot more natural than it feels. Regardless, make sure you feel comfortable with your look!

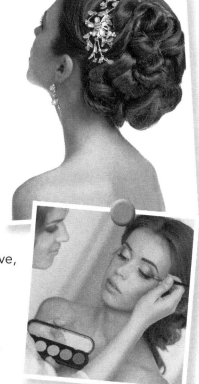

Flowers

Flowers add a luxurious feel to every wedding and you don't have to break the bank to have gorgeous garlands and beautiful buds adorn your venues.

Bridal bouquets, table centrepieces, buttonholes for groom and ushers are pretty standard at most weddings – and there are plenty of floral extras you may wish to consider depending on your budget.

 Varieties

Flowers which are in season when you marry are naturally always much cheaper than those which have to be flown in from afar so it's worth knowing what's in season during the year.

Spring

Agapanthus, Amaryllis, Anemone, Apple blossom, Bird of Paradise, Brodea, Calla lily, Cherry Blossom, Corn flower, Cosmose, Dahlia, Delphinium, Delwood, Forsythia, Freesia, Gardenia, Heather, Helleborus, Hollyhock, Hyacinth, Larkspur, Casa Blanca Lily, Gloriosa Lily, Stargazer, Liatrus, Lilac, Lisianthus, Narcissus, Orchid, Peach blossom, Peony, Phlox, Poppy, Protea, Pussy willow, Ranunculus, Rose, Seeded Eucalyptus, Solidago, Statice, Stephanotis, Stock, Sweet Pea, Tulip, Viburnum, Wax flower, Zinnia.

Summer

Alchemilla, Allium, Alstromeria, Amaranthus, Baby's Breath , Bird of Paradise, Calla lily, Campanula, Carnation, Chrysanthemum, Cockscomb, Cosmos, Dahlia, Delphinium, Dianthus, Didiscus, Euphorbia, Foxglove, Freesia, Gardenia, Genista, Ginger, Gladiolus, Hallaconia, Heather, Hydrangea, Hypericum, Iris, Kangaroo paw, Liatrus, Lilac, Casa Blanca

Autumn

Acashia, Allium, Alstromeria, Amaranthus, Anemone, Baby's Breath, Bittersweet, Carnation, China berry, Chrysanthemum, Cockscomb, Cosmos, Echinops, Freesia, Gerbera Daisy, Gladiolus, Hypericum, Iris, Juniper, Kangaroo paw, Kalancheo, Liatrus, Lily, Asiatic, Lily, Gloriosa, Misty Blue, Orchid, Pepper berry, Protea, Queen Ann's Lace, Quince, Rover, Roses, Rowen berry, Salvia, Solidago, Statice, Star of Bethlehem, Sunflower, Yarrow, Zinnia.

Winter

Acashia, Alstromeria, Amaryllis, Carnation, Chrysanthemums, Cyclamen, Evergreens, Gerbera Daisy, Ginger, Helleborus, Holly berry, Lily, Asiatic Lily, Casa Blanca Lily, Narcissus, Orchid, Pansy, Pepperberry, Phlox, Protea, Queen Ann's Lace, Roses, Star of Bethlehem, Statice.

Flowers don't just look, many varieties smell amazing too, and a pretty perfume can really add to the feel of your venue.

Table Centrepieces

After the bridal bouquet, and the bridesmaids if you have any, the flowers you are most likely to order are the centrepieces for your guest tables. Designs range from hugely decadent displays to subtly elegant posies. Here are a few ideas:

Boxed roses

Mirrored boxes filled with rose clusters, sometimes with diamanté pieces set into each rose. The box sits on a mirrored plate on which you can place tea lights which play off against the reflective surfaces.

Trumpet vases

Very tall vases (up to a metre) which are skinny and the base and wide at the neck. They're usually filled with large amounts of cascading flowers and foliage.

Fish Bowl

A great choice if you are doing the flowers yourself. You could add gel beads and fit a hand tied arrangement in the top or half fill the bowls with water, add some bear grass and then twist three or four gerberas inside for a simple yet effective design.

Mason Jars

Popular for vintage or summer weddings, these classic jars work well with traditional British summer flowers like sweet william, stocks, peonies and roses. Tie raffia or cute ribbons to work with your colour scheme.

The Florist

If you're going to use a florist always try to go with someone you've been recommended or who has an excellent reputation in the local community. Florists letting you down, delivering substandard produce or running late on the day are just not an option.

The average wedding flowers cost around £1000. **That generally includes all of the items below:**

Item	Price	Yes/No
Wedding party		
Bridal bouquet		
Bridesmaids bouquets		
Groom buttonhole		
Ushers buttonholes		
Flower girl basket		
Mothers corsages		
Fathers buttonholes		
Church/ Ceremony		
Altar		
Pews		
Entrance		
Reception		
Top table		
Table centrepieces		
Cake table		
Guest book table		
Other:		
Bouquets to hand out (mothers, helpers etc.)		

You might not need or want some of those pieces so ensure you give your florist a clear list of what's required and the times that you need them by. It's wise to have a written contract with your florist just in case anything goes wrong or you're not happy with the finished pieces. But to avoid this make sure you visit the shop and view some sample bouquets and arrangements at least a month prior to the wedding day.

You might not have budgeted for a florist and if you haven't don't worry because there's lots you can achieve with very little time or money.

Corsages

Instead of paying for bouquets for each bridesmaid why not have a corsage made? They are a fraction of the cost but still as pretty.

Tin cans

Wash out empty tin cans and remove the paper wrapping. These make cute little vases for shabby chic or country weddings. Or punch holes in them and add tea lights for a glimmering lantern look.

Plant pots

Paint terracotta plant pots to suit your theme and simply add a luscious green or flowering pot plant. Daisy plants in full bloom look sensational for a spring or summer wedding when set into aluminium buckets.

Hit the High Street!

Did you know that as well as plain wedding cakes, good old M&S now do a bridal flowers range? Order in advance and save a fortune!

Button bouquets

For the same price as a perishable flower bouquet, you can have beautiful bouquets made from buttons and ribbons – perfect for a vintage style wedding and something to keep forever!

The Alternative Touch

If you'd rather avoid the floral route altogether there are lots of other options you can use instead. For example:

Why not have helium balloons rather than floral centre pieces? They add height and really fill the room visually. The average price for a five piece table arrangement is £12.

Party planning shops have masses of choice with designs featuring wedding motifs like doves and hearts. A cute option is having coloured balloons inside transparent ones.

Instead of having floral garlands at the ceremony why not thread bunting along the seats or pews? You can also use it in the reception room, across the walls or to trim the tables.

Transport

Getting to and from your wedding and reception venues can be like a military operation and the journey should be considered when booking both venues because it could have a big budget impact.

Do you only need cars for the bridal party to the venue and that's it? Do they also need to wait through the service and take you on to the reception? Do you need one car for the bride and her father? Or several to cover the groom and ushers, bridesmaids, parents etc? The more cars you need, and the longer you need them for will obviously have a big impact on the cost, so plan carefully!

Traditional wedding cars like a Rolls Royce, Bentley or limousine can get booked up early in peak season, so make sure you look into it at least six months in advance.

Do you really need an expensive classic car for the bridesmaids, groom or even the bride? Given that all of your guests will already be inside the church waiting for you – no one will even see you arrive! Save the budget for other things!

Do you have a friend with a cool or classic car? Perhaps they could jazz it up with a giant bow or ribbon and act as your wedding car? Even the most normal cars will look great with a massive bow or floral display!

If you're worried about timings you may want to hire a big red bus or mini bus to take your guests – and maybe even you both too – from the church to the reception. It's a fun way for people to mingle and a great photo prop!

Ardley Village Hall is immediately on the right when you take the turn for Fritwell off the B430 (a quarter of a mile from M40 junction 10, approx 2 miles from Middleton Stoney).

There will be wine with supper but please bring a bottle of whatever you'd like to drink for the rest of the evening.

Top Tip

If your guests are making their own way to your venue make sure the directions are fail-safe. One bride had written on her invitations that the reception was being held at the town golf course. Only problem was that there were two golf courses... and quite a lot of guests went to the wrong one!

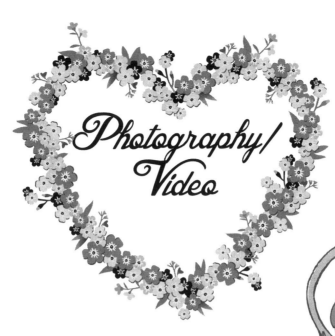

Photography/Video

You will obviously want to cherish the memories of your wedding day for years to come and be able to pass down images of you and your loved one to future generations. Choosing the right photographer is therefore one of the most important decisions you will have to make. With good research and planning you can find someone who you trust to do a good job and who offers the best value for money.

As well as asking friends for recommendations, it's always a good idea to attend local wedding fairs when looking for a wedding photographer because there will be a wide range on offer in one location, all of whom will be displaying their portfolios for you to see. Don't book on the day, but take cards and brochures so that you and your partner can sit down, look at their websites, and decide what style of photography you want after seeing all of the options.

Consider whether you want traditional, contemporary or reportage. Do you want black and white, sepia, colour or a mix of both? Black and white photographs have quite an old fashioned, romantic look to them and look lovely in displayed in a simple frame.

Photographers generally work to package deals but don't be afraid to negotiate and see if you can swap aspects of one package for another, or ask for a few extras. Packages tend to range from £500-£2000, and variations will include amounts of prints, photo albums and variety of media.

At the meeting you will get a feel for the person behind the lens. Go with your gut. If you get on with them, it's likely your guests will. It's no easy job trying to juggle 100 people on a busy wedding day and your photographer needs to be able to motivate, entertain and direct your guests.

Many good photographers will be able to show your images online and provide a link where you and your guests can view the images and order any prints they want directly.

There are also loads of great websites and apps that will allow all your guests to share their photos of your big day – all in one place. Your very own wedding app – how cool is that ?!

www.weddingphotoswap.com
www.trycapsule.com
www.wedpics.com
www.guestgallery.com

Here are a few questions to ask when meeting with photographers:

- How many weddings have they photographed before?
- Do they have previous examples of their work?
- What's their shooting style?
- Will they work to a brief?
- How long will they stay on the day?
- Have they worked at the venue before?
- Do they use digital or film cameras?
- Do they shoot in both black and white and colour?
- Will they have an assistant and will that cost extra?
- What is the overall cost?
- Do you need to pay them a deposit?
- Do you have to t pay for their travel/accommodation?
- Are any prints included in the fee or is every one extra?
- How much will it cost for friends and family to buy prints?
- Who retains the copyright?
- Will your pictures be used anywhere else, for instance on their website?
- Will you have to pay extra for an album?
- Can you see their T&Cs?
- Do they have insurance?

You'll go through a similar experience for hiring your videographer if you choose to have one. Make sure you check with the church or venue that filming is allowed.

The
Reception

The ceremony is over, the photos have been taken, and now it's time to eat, drink and be merry! Whether you're having a formal meal and speeches or a casual buffet and just a few short toasts, this is the time of the day that you get to spend time with your loved ones, share some great memories and hopefully and dance the night away to a few terrible disco classics.

Running Order

If you've already got an Order of Service for the ceremony you might want to include the reception details in that document as well and call it an Order of the Day instead.

A traditional reception running order looks something like this:

Welcome drinks/canapés

Photographs

Wedding meal

Speeches*

The cutting of the cake

The first dance

Evening entertainment /disco

Evening buffet

Speeches

Traditionally the speeches are given after the wedding breakfast, or during the dessert and coffees*, but more and more people are choosing to move them forwards, prior to the meal. If you're nervous about giving your speech this takes a bit of pressure off and means that you can relax and enjoy the meal afterwards without worrying that you'll have one too many glasses of fizz and end up slurring your words.

The order of speeches is usually as follows:

Bride's Father
Groom
Best Man

These days many brides and the father of the groom like to speak as well, to thank guests and such like. Much like the groom, it's also the bride's chance to say something publicly to her groom which is a little less formal than a wedding vow. You should do what you are most comfortable with, ensuring that no-one feels obliged to give a speech if they have a morbid fear of public speaking.

If you have a large amount of guests, make sure you've arranged with the venue to have a microphone – or arrange your own – because there's nothing worse than missing the punch-line of a joke. Plus if people are nervous they tend to speak quickly and words can easily missed.

Speeches are not just about humour and embarrassing the happy couple; they serve as an important way to thank all of the guests involved and they are also the time that gifts are often given out to the mothers of the bride and groom, bridesmaids, best man, ushers and any other contributors.

Say what?

Father of the Bride
He thanks the guests for coming, says a few words about his daughter, welcomes the groom to the family and proposes a toast to the happy couple.

The Groom
He thanks the father of the bride for his speech and the toast, says something about how happy he is to be married to his wonderful new wife, gives out thank-you gifts and proposes a toast to the bridesmaids.

The Best Man
Often the one the bride & groom are most nervous about! The best man thanks the groom on behalf of the bridesmaids for his kind words, tells anecdotes about the groom – sometimes including props or even a short film – and also proposes a toast to the bride and groom. Make sure he keeps it clean!

The Bride
Some brides write a poem, sing a song, tell a story about their partner and speak with, or just after, the groom.

Entertainment

During the wedding breakfast you may wish to have music playing quietly in the background or a wedding singer singing classic love songs while you eat. This is an added expense but it can be a beautiful addition that will impress your guests.

Generally after the meal guests move to another room – usually the bar – whist the venue changes the banquet room around for the evening. If it's dark outside at this point you may ask your guests to retire outside to watch a fireworks display or set off Chinese lanterns. You could have some games planned in the short time between the day and the evening guests arriving although form experience the daytime events often overrun and it's not unusual for punctual evening guests to arrive while the speeches are still running on! In good weather it's a lovely idea to plan something in a garden area to allow the guests to have some fresh air and stretch their legs.

If you have children attending they will be getting bored by this point so it's a great idea to book a children's entertainer to come in and occupy them for an hour or so, whilst the evening room is being set up. If you can't afford a professional why not ask a teenage daughter of a friend to come along and read some stories or play games like musical statues or pass the parcel?

Other ideas for entertainment which can bridge the gap from when your day guests finish their meals to the evening guests arriving:

- Casino tables
- Caricaturist
- Karaoke room
- String quartet in the garden area (this is also nice for the welcome drinks)
- Photo/Video booth

Let's Get This Party Started!

Once all of your evening guests have arrived you'll want to get the party started with a live band, wedding singer or DJ. Think about the type of atmosphere you want to create and don't stray too far from the tastes of you and your guests. After all it's your party!

Live Band

The great thing about live bands is that they are always gigging somewhere around the country so you can check them out beforehand and make sure you like them. Check them out on You Tube if they've uploaded videos. And don't be afraid to ask them if they take requests and can perform your first dance song.

Wedding Singer

If you've got the budget then a wedding singer is a nice start to the evening's entertainment, especially one who performs swing songs or other retro records and engages with the guests.

DJ

Check that your DJ has all of your favourite record choices by sending them a list beforehand. If you want an exact choice of songs or genres send that to them as soon as possible so it gives him an idea of what you're after.

Build your Own Playlist

A cheaper way of providing music is to use a PA system plugged into a pre-stocked music device. If your venue doesn't have one you can hire a very simple speaker system from your local audio visual hire company for about £100. Then you simply plug and play. You can pre-load an i-Pod or MP3 with your own music or create a playlist in iTunes or Spotify. The benefit to using iTunes is that you can fade the songs in and out so it feels like a proper disco.

Spotify gives you a budget busting amount of songs to choose from for just a one off monthly fee of around £7 which can be cancelled at any time. So if you only use it for a month then it costs you next to nothing.

First Dance

What will playing when you take to the dance floor?

 The first dance usually comes after the dinner and speeches have wrapped up, or at the start of the evening party, and even the most confident people can find it a bit nerve-wracking. Increasingly people are choosing to have dance lessons in the lead up to the big day, and practice does make perfect! Some people are even choreographing dance routines so their friends and family can join in. Whatever you decide to do, you want to make sure it's fun and stress-free.

Things to think about:

- Will you do a traditional slow dance or go up-tempo?
- Will you dance to a recorded track or will a band play it?
- Do you want guests to join you on the dance floor at any point? If so, let the DJ know or ask someone to announce it, or you could ask a few people to join you and allow everyone else to follow suit.

- Plan how you're going to end the dance. Will you take a small bow, stealthily slink off the dance floor or stay and groove to the next track?
- Do you just want one song, or one slow one followed by a fast-paced track to signal the start of partying?

If you're stuck for ideas for your first song, hopefully some of these favourites will inspire you!

Sade – *By Your Side*

Percy Sledge – *When a Man Loves a Woman*

Diana Ross and Lionel Ritchie – *Endless Love*

Eva Cassidy – *Songbird*

Tom Odell – *Grow Old With Me*

Queen – *You're My Best Friend*

Madonna – *Crazy For You*

Kiss – *I Was Made For Loving You*

Paul Weller – *You Do Something To Me*

Whitney Houston – *I Will Always Love You*

The Beach Boys – *God Only Knows*

Jackie Wilson – *Higher and Higher*

The Beatles – *Gotta Get You Into My Life*

James Blunt – *You're Beautiful*

Adele – *To Make You Feel My Love*

Elbow – *One Day Like This*

Elvis – *Can't Help Falling in Love*

Madness – *It Must Be Love*

Elton John – *The Way You Look Tonight*

James Morrison – *You Give Me Something*

Ellie Goulding – *How Long Will I Love You*

Evening Food

Depending on the budget you will need to decide what to offer your guests to eat in the evening, because those who ate at 4pm will be pretty peckish again by 9pm. See page 88 for more tips on evening food.

If you're at a hotel then your venue may include various options within the package you have chosen. These might include:

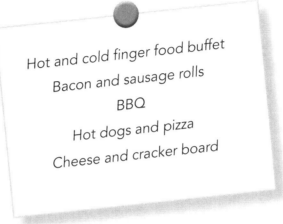

Hot and cold finger food buffet

Bacon and sausage rolls

BBQ

Hot dogs and pizza

Cheese and cracker board

If you can't afford to have any evening food then why not just put nibbles like crisps, peanuts and wedding cake out for the guests to snack on.

Extra, Extra

The weddings that you always remember the most are those that go the extra mile and provide special little details for their guests. Here are some ideas to think about:

- Cigars for after dinner
- Umbrellas and pashminas for guests who want to go outside
- A smoking area that is dressed and stocked with lighters and ashtrays
- Nice toiletries, soaps, tissues, perfumes and hairspray in the toilets
- A quiet room for older guests who don't want to leave early but prefer an area away from the crowds and loud music

Favours

It's been a tradition for some years now for guests to receive a small gift, called a 'favour', at their table during the wedding breakfast. It's a little token from the bride and groom to say thank you to each and every one of their friends and family.

Choosing your wedding favours is one of the most creative and fun decisions to make. A practical gift always goes down very well as does an edible or alcoholic one. There are heaps of ideas to suit every budget.

Sugared Almonds

Five sugared almonds were traditionally given to represent health, wealth, fertility, happiness and longevity. They were normally wrapped in voile sleeves and tied with ribbon but you can also use cute bags or boxes too.

Chocolates

Either in a cute gift box or in a voile bag. You can even get them with your new married name on.

Scratch Cards/Lottery Tickets

The great thing about buying a hundred or so scratch cards is that one of them is bound to win and if you get everyone to scratch them off at the same time it's a real treat to hear the squeaks of delight when they hit the jackpot. Or at least win a quid! Another option is a Lucky Dip lottery ticket for each guest, tie in fancy ribbon.

Other cute ideas: homemade jam (summer garden wedding), wedding cookies in a clear bag, cupcake in a box, personalised matches with a candle.

Sweetie Tables have become very popular over recent years. Buy cheap jars from Ebay and then hit your local cash and carry or market to stock up on all of your favourite childhood goodies! Provide each guest with a bag to fill and take home – or just enjoy that evening!

The
Final
Countdown

You've come so far and the big day is almost upon you. The week before the wedding can be exciting and stressful all wrapped in one exhilarating bundle but stay calm and have fun. Make sure you really enjoy the process instead of allowing things to stress you out!

Take the week off of work

This is good advice, otherwise you will find that you just don't have enough minutes in the day and won't be any use at work anyway because your head is in wedding mode!

Delegate

Don't feel overwhelmed by trying to do everything yourself. Get your fiancé, family, friends and bridesmaids involved too. Delegate, delegate, delegate:

- Confirmed final numbers with the venue?

- Make final payments all been made to suppliers/venues

- Create a Call Sheet and Contacts List (see overleaf) and issue a copy of this to everyone involved. This ensures everyone knows the running order, their arrival time and location, and has contact details for everyone involved. No one should be calling the bride on the day asking for a local taxi number! Also – ask your wedding car company for the name and mobile number of your driver – their office may be closed on a Saturday so you need to be able to call the driver direct if he is late or lost!

- Send a final running order with timings for everyone in the Wedding Party PLUS:

  Venue/caterer
  Florist
  Photographer/Videographer
  DJ/band
  Entertainers
  Transport provider
  Cake maker
  Any relevant Others

- Collect the wedding dress

- Collect any hired outfits

- Collect the wedding rings

- Run through the vows

- Practise the reception speeches

- Collect travellers' cheques and currency

- Pack for the honeymoon and book taxis

- Confirm play list to the DJ/band

- Confirm shot list to the photographer

- Wrap all thank-you gifts

- Get beauty treatments

- Enjoy a romantic dinner together

Have you have forgotten anything? It's good to have more than one pair of eyes so why not call a last minute meeting of all the bridesmaids, ushers and groom and go through the whole day step by step. That way everyone is on the same page and you can allocate any additional duties face to face.

Prepare a **'Wedding day essentials'** kit for yourself and give it to a trusted friend (not a bridesmaid as they won't be able to carry it with them on the day!). This will contain all the little things every bride will want to have close to hand.

Tissues
Pain relief
Clear nail polish
Mobile phone
Lipstick
Compact
Comb
Hairspray
Safety pins
Nail file
Breath mints
Plasters and heel grips
Make-up – for touch-ups
Blotting sheets – for shine

Sue & John Preston's Wedding

– Call Sheet & Contact Details
Friday June 24th

List of Contacts

Location/ Person	Address	Contact Person	Mobile Number
Church		Rev Simon Perkins	
Reception Venue		Sam Smith – Events manager	
Guildhall Classic Cars		Driver 1 (Bride): Driver 2 (Groom): Office:	
Bride's House		Sally Smith (mother of bride)	
Steve John's House (best man)		Steve John's House (best man)	
Hair		Jenny Shine	
Make-up		Sam Parker	
Florist			
Cake			
Photographer			
DJ			
Sue's Parents		Mum: Dad:	
John's Parents		Mum: Dad:	
Chief Bridesmaid		Justine Bell	
Venue – Local Taxi firms		Taxis Chelmsdale: Radio Cars Chelm:	

Call Sheet

Person	Arrival Time	Location	Contact Person
Bride's mum, bridesmaids	*8am*	*Sue's house*	
Hairdresser	*9am*	*Sue's house*	
Make-up	*9am*	*Sue's house*	
Fabbie Flowers- Buttonholes delivered	*10am*	*Steve John's House*	
Fabbie Flowers- Bouquets delivered	*10.30am*	*Sue's house*	
Fabbie Flowers – dress church	*11am*	*Church*	*Rev Simon Perkins*
Photographer	*11am*	*Sue's House (candid get ready shots)*	*Sally Smith*
Fabbie Flowers – Table flowers to venue	*1pm*		*Sam Smith, Venue Events Mgr*
Groom's Car	*1pm*	*John's House*	*Driver 1*
Father of the Bride	*1pm*	*Sue's House*	*Dad*
Bride's car	*1.30pm*	*Sue's House*	*Driver 2*
Cakes Couture	*1pm*	*Reception Venu*	*Sam Smith, Venue Events Mgr*
Swing Patrol (Band)	*7pm*	*Reception Venue (set-up after speeches)*	*Sam Smith, Venue Events Mgr*

After the Party

After months of planning you now need one last boost of organisation to ensure that everything you bought, booked and hired goes back to its rightful owner. When issuing jobs for the wedding party make sure that you also give them tasks for after the wedding because otherwise you'll find yourself doing it all on your lonesome.

Where possible have suppliers collect anything you've borrowed or hired. If you will be away on honeymoon, this may be at a family member's house, so it's crucial they are very clear on the exact address they are collecting from (which differs from where they delivered).

Make sure you know when the deadlines for returning items is because the last thing you want is to be charged for an extra days hire.

If you're relying on friends and family to pack down the whole wedding for your whilst you jet off on your honeymoon it's a wise idea to create a spreadsheet of all of the tasks in hand, with names, addresses, phone numbers and times due back. If they are collecting any cash deposits discuss where is the best place for this money to be held until you return.

Wedding Insurance

Not that we want to end on a boring note, but whether you're getting married at home or abroad, always, always take out wedding insurance. You never know what will happen with your event or your suppliers between the time you put down your deposit and your wedding day, so cover all possibilities by getting your wedding day insured.

Read the small print when considering which policy to buy because if the excess costs more than the claim it's not worth the paper it's written on. You will need specific insurance for weddings abroad, so make sure you get the right insurance for your event. You don't want to go to make a claim only to discover it was never covered in the first place.

And finally....

Other Books You May Like

Also by Alison McNicol:

The Wedding Table Plan Book:

The Fun and Easy Way to Cut Out and Design Your Perfect Wedding Seating Plan!

ISBN-13: 978-1908707307

Creating the perfect table seating plan for your wedding can be a complicated task – lots of trial and error – swapping around aunts, cousins, relatives and friends to create that perfect mix of guests at each table. But how to arrive at the perfect mix?

Forget about messy post-it's and names on bits of scrap paper, or even complicated computer programmes – **here's the fun and easy old-skool way to play your perfect wedding table seating plans!** Simply cut out each table in your room layout, cut out and fill in the name cards for all of your guests, then move them around as you play around with all the different options. Much more fun!

Turn the stressful task of organising your perfect wedding table seating plan into a fun game for you and your fiancé!

Every bride needs this book!

- Cut out and play around with: tables, name cards, room layouts and more!
- Tips on Top Table seating options – traditional or blended families.
- Round tables or rectangular? Tons of different room layout suggestions.
- Pages to list your initial guest list, and your final guest list and table plans.